VICTORIAN FURNITURE

The drawing room at 18, Stafford Terrace, London, furnished in the 1870s by Linley Sambourne, the famous *Punch* cartoonist. His family preserved the house almost unaltered and it has remained a typical example of a mid-Victorian town house. Photographs of several of the rooms appear in this book. The present owner, the Countess of Rosse, is Linley Sambourne's grand-daughter.

VICTORIAN FURNITURE

by

R. W. SYMONDS

and

B. B. WHINERAY

LONDON
COUNTRY LIFE LIMITED

First published in 1962
by Country Life Limited
2-10 Tavistock Street London WC2
Printed in Great Britain
by Hazell Watson & Viney Ltd
Aylesbury and Slough

© Executors of the late R. W. Symonds and
B. B. Whineray 1962

Contents

Illustrations

6

Illustrations

Illustrations

Victorian Furniture

Illustrations

Acknowledgments

I WOULD acknowledge the following for permission to reproduce photographs for which they hold the copyright. Their names are shown next to the appropriate photographs:

The Metropolitan Museum of Art, New York; The Victoria and Albert Museum; The Trustees of the Wallace Collection.

I would also like to acknowledge the Bodleian Library, Oxford, for permission to reproduce from the *House Decorator and Painter's Guide*, Figs. 6 and 8, and William Gordon Davies for Figs. 105 and 210.

Besides Messrs E. and N. Gibbs, who took the majority of the photographs, I would acknowledge the following:

F. J. Z. Carter for photographs of the Kenilworth Buffet. The Commercial Studios, Ipswich, for photographs taken at C. Silburn & Sons, R. W. Paul, Mrs Hammond and Green & Hatfield. Raymond Fortt for photographs supplied by Alec Lewis. Wallace Heaton for photograph of the desk, Fig. 33. L. H. Hildyard for photograph of the court cupboard, Fig. 12. Glyn Jones for photographs at Stradey Castle. Clifford V. Kendall for photograph of the chair, Fig. 271. Aubrey H. Leyland for photographs at Charlecote Park. A. C. K. Ware, Ltd. for photographs of the Chevy Chase sideboard.

B. B. W.

Preface

IT IS difficult to express the loss that students, collectors and dealers, interested in old English furniture, suffered by the death of Robert Symonds in September, 1958. So much was written and said at the time by his friends and associates that it is not easy to add anything new. Rarely in the field of English furniture has an understanding of design, coupled with an exact knowledge of construction, been found together in such a degree in one person.

Robert Symonds in his books has demonstrated that to have a full appreciation of period furniture many things must be considered. He realised that furniture could not be judged in isolation and that it was as important to know for whom and why it was made, as by whom and how; further, he thought it essential to understand the conditions and way of life for which the furniture was originally intended. It is, therefore, an especial tragedy that with his great knowledge of all aspects of period furniture and its production he was unable to carry through his project to write this book on Victorian furniture. It is the only period of English furniture not previously covered by his writings.

I myself was engaged by Robert Symonds in the early stages of this book to assist with the research, the selection of photographs and the preparation of the text. Much of the work was done at his house at Peasenhall in Suffolk. There, we were able, in spite of his failing health, to spend the day working on, or discussing, the book. Although at the time of his death it was far from complete and much research remained to be done, my close association with the work in the early phases made me feel that I was competent to carry out his expressed wish and continue the book.

Country Life Ltd were good enough to endorse Robert Symonds's opinion that I was qualified to continue and bring the work to completion. It cannot be pretended that it is as valuable as if he had been able to supervise it to the end; on the other hand, I hope the training and tuition that I received from Robert Symonds have enabled me not to deviate too far from his standard, which was the highest.

It is not always appreciated that there were as many changes and trends in furniture design in the reign of Queen Victoria as there had been in those of the previous five sovereigns. Therefore, in the space of some 50,000 words, this book can attempt only a general survey of Victorian furniture and its use and place in the Victorian home. Discussion of any one aspect in great detail has not been possible; the Exhibitions, wood-working machinery, papier mâché and the Arts and Crafts Movement, to name but a few, are all subjects, closely connected with furniture, which have been or could be expanded into works of their own. It is hoped, however, that enough has been said on each subject to give a balanced picture of furniture throughout the Victorian era.

The accession of Queen Victoria roughly coincided with significant changes in furniture styles. Therefore the limitation of discussion to the furniture of her reign poses little problem with regard to furniture styles before the year 1837.

The same cannot be said, however, of 1901, the year of the Queen's death. The most interesting furniture that was produced in the last twenty years of the reign was the work of individual designers and architects, many of them associated with the Arts and Crafts Movement. The trends which had started in the 1880s continued well into the 20th century, and to understand them fully they would have to be followed through to the close of the Edwardian era and often beyond. However, the leading designers, whose early work fell in the Victorian period, but who were to produce their most important and better known work after 1901, have been briefly mentioned.

Robert Symonds would, I know, have wished me to record his particular appreciation of the work done by his daughter, Mrs Virginia Rusack; this was a laborious but valuable study of many London and provincial magazines and newspapers from which she extracted information of considerable interest.

He would also wish to join me in acknowledging the help we received from the late Peter Floud. Floud had a great and wide knowledge of the period; in the field of furniture he had done much important work, particularly with the dating of furniture trade catalogues; we benefited from his knowledge by reading his published works and by many pleasant talks with him, when he was unstinting with his help and advice.

The Exhibition of Victorian and Edwardian Decorative Arts, which was organised under Peter Floud's direction by the Victoria and Albert Museum in 1952, was perhaps the most important single event that helped to awaken the public's interest in Victorian furniture. The catalogue of this Exhibition published by H.M. Stationery Office is a mine of information. With this Exhibition, people began to realise almost for the first time that the vague general term 'Victorian', when applied to 19th-century furniture, had about as much significance, and the same lack of meaning, as 'Georgian' when applied to 18th-century furniture.

It will be a tragedy if the Victoria and Albert and other museums delay further in opening galleries for 19th-century Decorative Arts. Now is the time to stimulate interest and encourage understanding and to save much that is at present unappreciated or unrecognised. The Victorian Society is attempting to do for its period what the Georgian Society has done so admirably for the 18th century. Anyone with an interest in the Victorian era should not fail to give to the Society his full support, to enable it to take action to preserve so much that is important and of interest and which is being continually threatened.

I have received nothing but help and kindness from the many people with whom I have come into contact while working on this book. Often they have gone to great lengths to answer my questions and to make available their houses and furniture for photographing; in this respect a number of antique dealers have been particularly helpful. I would like to extend to all these people my most grateful thanks. The owner of each piece of furniture is shown by the appropriate illustration. There are, however, a few exceptions; these are photographs which were in Robert Symonds's possession and about which I have no information. I am sorry that I have been unable to acknowledge the owners and I trust that they will forgive the unavoidable omission and accept my apologies and thanks.

I must mention by name the following who have been most especially kind, either with help or in allowing an unusual amount of their furniture to be photographed, or in supplying me with specialised information:

Mr G. R. Batho, for information about Gerrard Robinson.

Mr Philip Blairman, for allowing various pieces in his private collection to be photographed.

Mr John Bonython of Crafers, South Australia, for sending several photographs of chairs bearing Victorian London furniture makers' labels.

Mr Christopher Cory, for a very useful suggestion and for taking the photograph of Stradey Castle.

The family of the late Mr John Crace, for allowing me access to their family papers.

Mr John Gloag, for permission to reproduce various photographs and giving some welcome advice about the manuscript.

Mrs Hammond of Benacre Hall, Suffolk, for allowing her furniture to be photographed.

The Marquess and Marchioness of Hertford, for the photographs from Ragley Hall.

Mr Thomas Howarth, the author of *Charles Rennie MacKintosh and the Modern Movement*, for permission to reproduce a photograph of the drawing room at Dunglass Castle.

Mrs Wallace Hughes, for allowing her fine collection of papier mâché to be photographed and for giving me some interesting information about these pieces.

Mr J. T. W. James of Holland and Sons, Mount Street, London, for much valuable information both from the papers and accounts of his firm and from his personal recollections.

Mr D. W. Kendall, for providing much information about Kendalls of Warwick and allowing me to reproduce some designs from his family's papers.

Mr George J. Levy, for allowing various pieces in his private collection to be photographed.

Mr Alec Lewis, for allowing many of his pieces to be photographed and for much interesting information.

Sir Geoffrey Mander, for the contemporary photograph of the 'Great Parlour' at Wightwick Manor.

Mr and Mrs C. R. Mansel Lewis and Mr David and Lady Mary Mansel Lewis, for photographs and information about Stradey Castle.

Mrs Elfrida Mostyn, for providing me with two photographs of furniture at Abney Hall and some interesting information about the Crace family.

Mr. A. B. C. Philips, for permission to use the photographs of his circular dining table at The Heath House, Tean, Staffs.

Mr C. R. N. Routh, Curator of Charlecote Park (the property of the National Trust), for help and information about the dining room sideboard and other furniture.

Alderman Miss E. M. Thornton, for allowing her fine collection of furniture made by Holland and Sons to be photographed, at considerable inconvenience to herself.

The Earl of Warwick, for permission to photograph the Kenilworth Buffet and for information about this piece supplied by his Agents.

The coloured frontispiece of this book and several other photographs included in the text have been taken at 18, Stafford Terrace, London. This house has remained virtually unaltered since 1874 when it first became the home of Linley Sambourne, the famous *Punch* cartoonist. The house passed to his daughter, Mrs Messel, who preserved it almost exactly as her father had furnished it. The present owner, the Countess of Rosse, is Linley Sambourne's grand-daughter, and I am very much indebted to her for considerable help and for allowing extensive photography at Stafford Terrace.

Three people often assisted Robert Symonds and continued to give me their help, for which I am grateful. They are Mr Robert Langhorn, the cabinet maker, whose advice and knowledge has contributed considerably to the interest of the chapter on Techniques and Materials; and Messrs E. and N. Gibbs, the commercial photographers, who have taken a great number of the photographs and whose expertise has produced such excellent results.

The staff at the Victoria and Albert Museum and the London Library have been, as always, courteous and efficient.

I am indebted to Mrs Florence Smart for her patience and help in connection with the photographs and for valuable assistance with the preparation of the captions.

Lastly, I must thank Mrs Barr and Mrs Kenneth Barley, who helped Robert Symonds so much in the last months in London and at Peasenhall; without them he would not have been able to take the book even part of the way.

B. B. Whineray

Spurstow Hall,
Cheshire

CHAPTER ONE

From Craft to Industry

THE RADICAL changes in furniture design that came with the 19th century were accounted for to a great extent by the altering social and economic conditions of the country. These changes in furniture, though gradual at first, were by the accession of Queen Victoria well established, little of the 18th century remaining, either in style or method of production.

The rise in population, the increase of wealth and the change in its distribution, the introduction of machinery and the vastly improved conditions of transport were all factors at variance with the conditions that produced the old traditional system of craftsmanship. These new influences not only affected the design and craftsmanship of furniture, but also its distribution and marketing.

Instead of the old need to provide the best for a comparatively limited cultured society, there came the demands of a new vital bourgeoisie, whose members as the century advanced were competing to outdo each other in the visible presentation of their success. Such a change did not happen overnight and the first two decades of the 19th century still saw a continuation of the traditional system of handicraft. Thereafter, greatly increased production, helped by the use of wood-working machinery, had the inevitable consequence of separating the maker from the customer. Until 1800 the craft of furniture making had altered fundamentally very little throughout the centuries and tradition was the all-important factor in the handicrafts from mediaeval times to the end of the 18th century. It guided the craftsman in every aspect of his trade; it taught him the use of his tools, the advantages and limitations of his material and how these combined with the requirements of his time to influence construction and design.

In a traditional age, such as the 18th century, the skilled craftsman, whether he was a joiner, a cabinet-maker or silversmith, could not go far astray and he was never at a loss for the design of his wares. Because of these conditions a cabinet-maker made his furniture in accordance with the standard designs which were common at the time to the whole of the furniture handicraft. It was for this reason that in the 18th century the proportions and general design of furniture did not vary to any great extent, even when pieces such as chests of drawers, bureaux, book cases and dining tables were made in widely different parts of England; there were some local variations in ornament and occasionally in style, which are discussed later. The craftsman seldom had reason to invent novel and extravagant designs—although there were exceptions, of course—to tempt his customers; they were quite happy to buy the contemporary furniture designed in accordance with the social requirements of the time.

Victorian Furniture

Earlier centuries saw a series of different styles follow each other in succession; an old style's influence gradually grew weaker, as that of the new style grew stronger, for the change was never dramatic. Each style had its own ornament, but a style did not consist of ornament alone, for it included the shape, and often the proportions, of the structure upon which the ornament was applied. With English furniture a chest of drawers or commode in the Baroque period was rectangular in plan; in the Rococo it was serpentine; in the neo-classic it often became half-circular. Chairs in the first half of the 17th century had low backs; in the last half they had high backs. These were standard shapes adopted by most cabinet and chair makers, and the ornament—which was at the discretion of the craftsman—was seldom applied in bad taste.

The newest fashions always appeared in the capital, and there was an inevitable time-lag between London fashion and that of the provincial towns. There was also variation between furniture made in different parts of the provinces, but this applied more to the furniture of the 16th and 17th centuries, when some regions had certain peculiarities of design, most often noticeable in the ornament. Chairs were particularly affected; Yorkshire and Lancashire had their own types of chair and all north country chairs were of a sturdier and stronger build than those of the south. As the 18th century advanced and books showing furniture designs were published and road transport improved, the variations in regional design grew less marked.

The problems of supply and demand were not complicated. In furniture making the supply revolved around the unit of the master craftsman of whom there were a large number throughout England: many such craftsmen were owners of small businesses employing journeymen and two or more apprentices. Every master had his own particular handicraft, and therefore he specialised in the making of certain types of furniture.

Joiners made furniture in the solid wood (often of oak when it was termed 'wainscot'); cabinet-makers made veneered furniture; chair-makers specialised in stools and couches as well as chairs. Then there was the individual craft of the upholsterer who stuffed the frames of chairs and couches and also made beds and curtains.

In the first half of the 18th century, the average cabinet- or chair-maker's establishment was small, and the master craftsman lived with his family and apprentices above his workshop in the same way as his forebears had done. As the century advanced, however, some master craftsmen became more successful than others and their businesses expanded. This was especially the case with those London masters who had obtained the patronage of the wealthy. It became the tendency for the various furniture crafts to coalesce. A joiner and a cabinet-maker would go into partnership, thus allowing a larger range of furniture to be made and thereby giving the business an increase in turnover and profit.

In London, a cabinet-maker and an upholsterer (a very favoured combination) would not only make book cases, tables, upholstered chairs and couches and beds, but would also employ carvers and gilders—the craftsmen who made gilt furniture and looking glass frames. Some cabinet-makers also dealt in glass; they bought the rough-cast glass plates from the glasshouse and employed workmen who polished and silvered them for looking glasses. They also made panels for coach windows.

This gathering together under one roof of a number of ancillary trades was a natural tendency of ambitious masters. The go-ahead master craftsman, among his other activities, also carried out the role of shopkeeper, for he found that he could make a profit by buying the wares of other craftsmen and selling them retail. A significant feature of the latter half of the 18th century was this growth of firms, whose partners were both craftsmen and shopkeepers, and who could accordingly supply their customers with the complete furnishing and decoration of a house. From the bills of Chippendale, we know that he sold his customers not only cabinet-ware, chairs, looking glasses and upholstered beds, but also wall-paper and carpets.

An indication of the way in which the businesses of furniture makers expanded in the last half of the 18th century, and how the number of their journeymen increased, can be gauged from the newspaper accounts describing the burning down of a firm's premises—a not un-common event in the days when oil lamps and candles were the only form of lighting and an open fire or stove the only form of heating.

There is such an account of the burning of Thomas Chippendale's workshop and the loss of the tool chests of twenty-two journeymen. In 1768, George Seddon, 'the eminent cabinet-maker of London', whose workshops were at London House, Aldersgate Street, was the victim of a fire which destroyed the house as well as adjoining buildings, 'besides an immense quantity of cabinet goods, and upwards of eighty chests of tools'. In 1783 another fire occurred at Sed-don's workshops. The following report is from the *Norfolk Chronicle* of November 8th, 1783:

'All Mr Seddon's very extensive workshops are consumed . . . Among the unfortunate sufferers are Mr Seddon's journeymen, near 300 in number, each of whom, according to the custom of the trade, found his own tools, and all those belonging to Mr Seddon's workmen are destroyed. A chest of cabinet tools is worth from five to fifty pounds, and as Mr Seddon employed the most capital hands, the loss in tools only is very great, and must be an event highly distressing to a great number of families.

'Among the valuable articles destroyed by the dreadful conflagration at Mr Seddon's was a plate of glass, the manufacture of this kingdom, intended for the Empress of Russia.'

The evidence of these two fires shows how much Seddon's business must have expanded within fifteen years, the number of journeymen he employed having increased during this time by 220 men.

The diary of Sophie von la Roche contains an account of this German lady's visit to Seddon's warehouse in 1786. What is interesting is the large amount of household furniture set out for sale in the various showrooms:

'We drove first to Mr Seddon's . . . He employs four hundred apprentices [journeymen and apprentices] on any work connected with the making of household furniture—joiners, carvers, gilders, mirror-workers, upholsterers, girdlers—who mould the bronze into graceful patterns—and locksmiths. All these are housed in a building with six wings. In the basement mirrors are cast and cut. Some other department contains nothing but chairs, sofas and stools of every description, some quite simple, others exquisitely carved and made of all varieties of wood, and one large room is full up with all the finished ar-ticles in this line, while others are occupied by writing-tables, cupboards, chests of drawers, charmingly fashioned desks, chests, both large and small, work- and toilet-tables in all manner of wood and patterns, from the simplest and cheapest to the most elegant and expensive.'

19

Victorian Furniture

This display of wares for sale extended to other branches of trade; for instance, Wedgwood and Byerley had a showroom in York Street, St James's Square, at the beginning of the 19th century, in which was shown an extensive collection of pottery wares made by the firm which was founded by Josiah Wedgwood. These retail showrooms or 'magazines', as they were also called, were an innovation of the late 18th century and the forerunners of the large London stores whose names today have become household words.

The growth in furniture production and expansion of its retail trade went hand in hand with the rise in population. In 1702, when Queen Anne came to the throne, the population of England and Wales was 5½ millions; by the turn of the century it had risen to 9 millions. This increase, though considerable, was nothing compared with what was to come. In the next thirty years the population of England and Wales rose to nearly 14 millions and by the year of the Great Exhibition—1851—it was nearly 18 millions, and the rise continued.

During the first thirty years of the 19th century—the transitional period between Georgian and Victorian England—the wealth of the country had also greatly increased and had become distributed through a wider section of the community. In 1800 the official value of Britain's exports was £34,000,000; by 1830 the value had more than doubled, and by the middle of the century it was standing at £197,000,000. This advance in the national wealth created in its train a rich bourgeois class and an improvement in the well being of the now growing middle class.

In the 18th century the leading nobility and landed gentry patronised the London craftsmen and shopkeepers. Their coaches, their gold and silver plate, their jewellery, their clothes, and their furniture were bought in London. In the 19th century the demand for these wares increased, because the new bourgeoisie copied the upper classes and likewise patronised the London craftsmen and shopkeepers.

This greater demand put a strain on to the old and tried methods of hand craftsmanship, and this was especially true of furniture production. The most important London firms of furniture makers now became busier than ever before. They enlarged their premises, took on more employees, and modernised their workshops by the introduction of wood-working machines. They found that the new rich, with their different criteria, were easier to please than their more aristocratic patrons; the more comfortable and opulent looking the furniture, the more it appealed to their new customers' taste.

Further evidence of the size and activities of some of the principal London firms is to be found in an account written in 1877 by a certain G. Hungerford Pollen:

'The number of hands employed in large cabinet-making and furnishing establishments is very considerable. Not only are the workshops well provided with joiners, cabinet-makers and turners, but also with upholsterers, cutters-out and work-women, stuffing, tacking on or sewing on the covers of chairs, sofas, etc. Indeed, it is no uncommon occurrence for the entire furniture of royal palaces and yachts to be ordered from one of these firms by the courts of foreign potentates in every corner of the world. Chairs, tables, sideboards, etc. were made lately at Messrs Holland's for a steam yacht of the Emperor of Austria; whilst Messrs Jackson and Graham have been furnishing the palace of the Grand Khedive at Cairo.'

The writer goes on to say that in order to execute large orders it was necessary that the firm had at its command a number of first-rate craftsmen. For instance, the firm of Jackson and Graham had 600 to 1,000 work-people, according to the time of the year and the pressure of orders and their weekly wage bill was nearly £2,000.

Gillows of Lancaster are a good example of a firm that prospered and increased under the new conditions. In 1761 Robert Gillow had formed a London branch of the firm and it is recorded that by 1887 they employed over 500 men.

These figures of employees show a continual rise from the late 18th century, when Seddon had 300 journeymen, to the 1870s when Gillows had 500 and Jackson and Graham 600 to 1,000 employees. In view of the growth of the population and the prosperity of the country, it is possible that this increase may not seem as large as one would expect. What must not be forgotten, however, is that the large 19th-century firm was using a number of labour-saving devices in the shape of wood-working machinery and that its work was not all executed by hand as it had been in the days of Seddon. Evidence of the use of machinery at Jackson and Graham's is provided by Sir Matthew Digby Wyatt, the architect and first Slade Professor of Fine Arts at Cambridge, in his official report on the Paris Exhibition of 1855:

> 'A steam engine, and machinery for various purposes connected with cabinet-making, have recently been erected and put into operation, by which means a considerable saving is effected in production, without any diminution of wages.'

A sign of the prosperity in the manufacture of Victorian furniture is revealed by the census figures of the numbers of persons in the cabinet-makers' and upholsterers' trades. In 1851 we find 40,897 persons employed in these two occupations, but by 1871 this figure had risen to 56,945—as clear an indication as any of the growth of an industry.

Furniture did not lend itself to mass production in a factory except when quantities of an identical article were required. The first article of English furniture to be mass produced was the cheap chair with turned legs and a wooden seat; a large and constant demand for such a chair began in the 18th century. In due course this brought about its mass production by a number of firms. There were two chair factories at Hammersmith in the early part of the 19th century. 'A very great number of those wooden chairs, known by the designation of Windsor chairs, are made here [Hammersmith] together with rustic seats, etc. by Webb and Bruce, and Mr Carter.'

The well-known Windsor chair was much favoured and manufactured in large numbers in the late 18th and through the 19th century (Fig. 123) and even today it has not gone out of production.

One notable difference was that the showroom and the factory producing it had now become separate entities, as we learn from an advertisement in the *Furniture Gazette* of January 1st, 1876, of John Jones & Son—'Wholesale and Export Cane Seat and Windsor Chair Manufacturers'. Their showrooms were at 95, Curtain Road, London, E.C. and their 'manufactory' at High Wycombe, Bucks. Similarly, A. Stone & Son—'Wholesale and Export Cane, Windsor, and Willow Seat Chair Manufacturers'—of High Wycombe had their London showrooms and offices at 328, Old Street, E.C. High Wycombe had for several centuries been an important centre for chair-making because the great beech woods in the locality provided a ready supply of the required timber.

Victorian Furniture

The separation of the factory from the showroom, although it was a notable feature of the trade during the century, was not in itself a 19th-century innovation. This division of a business into two components, making for greater efficiency in each, had already started in the furniture trade during the latter years of the 18th century. Sir Ambrose Heal, in *London Furniture Makers, 1660–1840*, mentions among others Charles Pryer, Cabinet-maker and Upholsterer, whose shop was at 472, Strand, but whose 'manufactory' was in Paradise Row, Chelsea.

Cheap, painted, softwood furniture, often for bedrooms and kitchen chairs and tables, was very suitable for mass production and these were the first types of furniture to be made in large quantities in factories. They were seldom sold direct to the customer, but were marketed through shopkeepers.

The divisions between the various furnishing trades in the Victorian era are described in an account on 'furniture' in the official catalogue of the Paris Universal Exhibition of 1867. This account shows how Victorian firms followed the earlier practice of the 18th century, but in a much bigger way, when a craftsman in one trade dealt retail in wares made by another. The writer says:

'All the principal furniture makers, who have given real importance to their trade, have experienced considerable advantage by adding to it the sale of everything connected with decoration and ornament; and with very few exceptions, their establishments undertake upholstery as well. On the other hand, the best upholsterers manufacture or commission the manufacturers to make for them, in their name, all kinds of elegant furniture and cabinet work. It is the same in the case of beds and bedding, now made by manufacturers of furniture as well as by upholsterers.'

These important furniture makers were at the top of their trade and they made the most expensive cabinet and upholstered wares for fashionable and wealthy clients.

The bulk of the furniture trade, however, was busy working for a different social strata, not so wealthy but far greater in numbers. The middle classes were the cause in the first half of Victoria's reign for so much of the new building taking place both in London and the provincial towns and cities. The new villas and houses varied from two storeys to four or five, including the inevitable basement, and when one considers the miles of new streets built in London alone, it is not surprising that so much Victorian furniture exists.

The retail supplier of furniture to the middle-class home ranged from the furnishing store, which sold everything, to the cabinet-maker's establishment, which specialised in furniture and beds and bedding only. An advertisement in 1867 by the furnishing store, Atkinson & Co. of Westminster Bridge Road, is worded in the traditional 18th-century style; they 'beg to announce to the Nobility, Gentry, Clergy' (but it is all important to notice that they now add) 'and the general Public, that they have enlarged their premises for the better display of their Stock'.

The Stock consisted of 'Drawing-Room Furniture, a large number of Marqueterie Cabinets, Oval and Loo Tables, Davenports, and What-Nots'. Also 'Good Solid Dining-Room Sets in Oak and Mahogany, Brass and Iron Bedsteads, in great variety, and from very low prices', and a 'New Patent Spring Mattress' is also listed. The advertisement states that 'the whole of the bedding is made on the premises and under personal inspection'. Furnishing Drapery, Bed and

Table Linen, Damask, Rep and Pekin Cloths, Chintzes and Muslin Lace Curtains were also stocked, together with Carpets, Floor Cloth, Linoleum and Cork Carpet.

Many of these shops supplying the middle classes did not make the furniture they sold, but bought it from wholesale firms of cabinet and chair makers who supplied the trade. In the East End of London there were many small individual businesses of cabinet- and chair-makers and upholsterers who, in their advertisements in the *Furniture Gazette* and other trade journals, described themselves as 'wholesale'. Examples were:

Brew and Claris, 1, South Place, London, E.C.
'Wholesale and export cabinet-makers and upholsterers.'

S. Mason, Upholsterer and Cabinet-Maker, 97, Curtain Road, London, E.C.
'The Trade Supplied on the Most Reasonable Terms consistent with quality.'

A letter to the *Furniture Gazette* (Oct., 1875) is illuminating on the source of supply to what the writer, an Edinburgh cabinet-maker, terms the 'first-class West End houses'. In the beginning of this letter he discusses the designs of furniture applicable to the *Gazette* and goes on to say:

'With respect to your Original Design for high-class and costly Furniture, this can only be approved of by first-class West End houses, which are few in number, and do not appear to support your journal by advertising in it. These houses will disapprove of your giving designs from the real manufacturers, as they assert that all the goods they sell are either made by themselves or to their order. This, as is known to anyone acquainted with the trade, is not the case; with very few exceptions they are all supplied from the East End of London, which they affect so much to despise, although their conveyances are daily seen in the neighbourhood taking away goods, to say nothing of the visits of the buyers for the purpose of purchasing.

'The East End of London is hourly improving in the manufacture of furniture, and goods of the first quality can be obtained there. The country dealers also flock to that mart for all their supplies . . .'

The 'West End houses' mentioned in the above letter were not the few high-class establishments such as Jackson and Graham, but more general furnishing shops. The proprietors of these shops, as the writer of the above letter confirms, conveyed to the general public the impression that the furniture which they sold was of their own design and make.

A large and enterprising factory or 'Cabinet Warehouse' was that of William Smee & Sons. This firm carried on both a wholesale and a retail business; as wholesale furniture makers they were probably one of the largest firms to supply the trade in the early Victorian period. In order to make it easier for shopkeepers to buy and sell their furniture, they distributed printed catalogues, which had no title page with the name of Smee, but on the inside of the back cover was pasted a printed sheet which read: 'Designs of Furniture by William Smee & Son, a Stock of which is always kept ready for Sale, at their Cabinet and Upholstery Manufactory and Warerooms No 6, Finsbury Pavement, London.'

The authors have seen such a catalogue with Smee's name and address blotted out by printed slips pasted over them, and the sheet amended to read that the furniture was 'Manufactured by H. Thompson, 116 Long Acre, London.' The inclusion of the words 'Manufactured by' shows that Thompson was particularly anxious that his customers should think that he was the actual maker. The catalogue has 324 pages of line-engraved designs for domestic furniture of all types, ranging from chairs, sideboards, tables and bedroom furniture to what-nots, butler's trays, Windsor chairs, and hat and umbrella stands. Many of the pieces are described as 'french polished', and another description is 'Superior', indicating that some of the furniture was of better quality than others (Fig. 1).

As has already been shown, an important difference between furniture making of the 18th century and that of the 19th century was that in the former age a master cabinet-maker generally sold his wares direct to his customer, but with the advent of the shopkeeper, who sold but did not manufacture, the link between the cabinet-maker and the customer was broken. No longer could the former learn at first hand what the latter wanted. Thomas Chippendale thought little of a five-day journey by coach to see a customer, and many must have been the occasions when customers visited his workshop at St Martin's Lane to inspect the furniture he was making for them. What was clumsy in design was pointed out and amended, and a pleasing shape was further improved by apt criticism. The fashionable 18th-century cabinet-maker owed much to the cultured upper classes for their intuitive knowledge of what was in good taste.

Another difference between the furniture of the master craftsman of the 18th century and the 'ready made furniture' displayed in a furniture shop of the 19th century was that the former made his furniture for immediate use by the customer, whereas the shopkeeper's stock was held ready for sale to a wide range of customers. Such conditions meant that a customer buying furniture in a retail shop, which sold but did not make, had no say over the design, for he had to accept what the shopkeeper showed him. He could not ask for the shape of a chair to be altered or a piece of carving to be omitted, for this would entail making a special chair the cost of which would be greatly in excess of the stock design.

Each wholesale cabinet- and chair-maker, who supplied the shopkeepers, had stock designs which simplified and cheapened production, and to alter a stock design was now impractical. These wholesale firms had neither direct contact with the customer, which could allow them to know what his tastes and requirements were, nor had they any traditional design to guide them. The manufacturers now came to rely upon rich ornament to help them in the problem of making their furniture pleasing and saleable. Ornament to many Victorians was the beginning and end-all of design.

In provincial towns there were still firms of cabinet- and chair-makers and upholsterers who sold their products in the 18th-century way. That each town other than a village depended upon its local furniture makers and upholsterers is evident by the number of these craftsmen that appear in Victorian directories. At Kingston-upon-Hull in 1846 there were 37 cabinet-makers and upholsterers, who supplied the wants of a population of 66,000 odd. Besides the cabinet-makers there were 30 furniture brokers. In the City of York in 1841 there were 36 cabinet-makers and upholsterers, 9 carvers and gilders, 2 chair-makers and 20 furniture brokers. The population of York was only 28,842.

The furniture broker was the dealer in second-hand furniture. The number of brokers in Hull and York suggests that selling second-hand furniture in these two provincial cities was as important as the making and selling of new furniture. The re-use of second-hand wares by people of a lower social level is a factor that cannot be overlooked by the furniture historian of the Victorian age.

The small firms of cabinet-makers and upholsterers supplying the local demands of a country town were the last stronghold of making furniture in the traditional way. The provincial directories are evidence that they continued in business at least until the end of Victoria's reign, when the large wholesale factory's mass-production methods made provincial furniture making in small workshops without machinery uneconomic.

The same thing was happening throughout the country in other trades. Small businesses in both London and the provinces such as boot-makers, tailors, stay-makers and hatters and dressmakers gave up their shops with the coming of mass production of their wares in factories, and the establishment of chain stores which sold these commodities. This did not apply, however, to the best London furniture makers any more than to the firms who made the highest quality goods in other fields—this type of firm is still in existence today.

Another aspect of Victorian furniture making is the export trade which was an additional source of income to the London cabinet-makers and upholsterers. There was nothing new in the export of furniture, for ever since the late 17th century English joiners, cabinet-makers and upholsterers had been exporting their wares not only to Europe, but also to the American colonies.

Evidence of the furniture export trade in Victorian times is to be found in contemporary advertisements. In the *Furniture Gazette* (July 10th, 1875) one James Dagleish advertises as 'a wholesale and export Looking-glass and Cabinet Manufacturer, Gilder, Plate Glass Factor, and Silverer', and calls the attention of 'the Trade and Shippers to his large and well-assorted stock of every description of Cabinet and Upholstered Goods'.

Edward Coote also advertises that he is 'a Wholesale and Export Cabinet Manufacturer and Upholsterer' and is 'well known in the Trade to be one of the best Designers and Manufacturers of substantial and seasoned Furniture in London, and warrants all his goods to bear the test of any climate'.

We get a glimpse of the English furniture export trade from an account written by the American Trade Bureau, published in February, 1875. This account complains of the lack of enterprise of the American furniture trade for exporting its products:

> 'When we consider the fact that mahogany is sent from San Domingo, Honduras and Mexico to England, made into furniture and then re-shipped to the West Indies, Brazil, Argentine Republic, Peru and other South American States, passing our very doors in transit, it seems as if we should exert ourselves a little more to extend a trade that is legitimately ours. One of the first remarks that will be offered in reply to the statement that England controls so much of the South American trade, will be that with her cheap labour she can produce, sell and deliver at a less price than we can.'

The writer goes on to say that although American labour is more expensive, their more general use of machinery should offset this. He also points out that the best timber is cheaper in the United States.

The Bureau also comments upon the safe and rapid transport to South America by the three-masted schooners now so popular. However, the lack of enterprise on the part of the Americans did not last for long and in 1882 the *Furniture Gazette* reports 'A London Depot of American Furniture'. It would appear that previously there had been no sale for American-made furniture in England because the designs were not in accordance with English requirements. But W. Angus & Co., of Finsbury, E.C., realised this deficiency and accordingly arranged to have the imported furniture made to suit the English market. When this was done the prejudice against American furniture died out and it found a ready sale.

The American furniture was packed like 'solid timber' to save transport costs and it was fitted and finished on its arrival in England. One of the American specialities was 'Rattan' or cane furniture, which was sold to the public by several London West End houses.

French furniture was fashionable with the English upper classes, and the amount annually imported probably equalled that of the English furniture exported to France. In 1881 the French levied a new tariff on imported furniture and carpets and this was looked upon as a serious handicap to English manufacturers. Swiss and Belgian furniture also found a market in England; in 1887 Cawley Morris & Co., of City Road, advertised that they were importers of this furniture as well as French. There appeared an advertisement of Danish furniture in the *Art Journal Catalogue* of the International Exhibition of 1867: 'Some choice specimens of Cabinet and Upholstery Furniture, Grand Pianos and Terra Cotta'. It was imported and sold by Nosotti's, of Oxford Street, who advertised that it was under the patronage of the Princess of Wales, later Queen Alexandra, who was Danish by birth.

'Native-made Indian Furniture' and 'Carved Blackwood Furniture', which came direct from India, found a ready sale in England and a number of English firms imported it. That this trade both with Indian and Chinese blackwood furniture was very active in the last half of Victoria's reign is evident by the great quantity of it that is to be found today.

The various activities of the East End furniture trade have been described in the foregoing pages, but no special mention has yet been made of the cheap furniture which was produced for homes of people of the lowest income group. Many East End wholesale firms specialised in the making of very cheap furniture, which they sold through the medium of shopkeepers whose establishments were in the poorest parts of London.

The very low price of this furniture was brought about by the use of inferior materials poorly finished—beech instead of walnut, varnished surfaces instead of polished, upholstery stuffed with flock, pig hair and even hay and seaweed instead of curled horse hair, and seats and backs of stuffed chairs with too few springs, and these of poor quality. Quite apart, however, from the use of inferior and rubbishy material, the East End trade in cheap furniture had earned itself an unsavoury reputation in another way. Under the heading of 'Slaughter House Furniture' an account of this trade is given by a writer in the *Eastern Post*:

'I occasionally, on Saturday afternoons, take a walk through the great furniture market of East Central London, and my heart bleeds at the scenes I witness of the degradation which a once splendid trade suffers in the persons of manufacturing operatives, cabinet, chair, and sofa-makers. Fine furniture is made, and is on show in the warehouses of Curtain Road, but I am sorry to say much flimsy furniture is also to be obtained there, to suit, of course, the pockets of a certain class of people. It is, however, the exhibitions and the scenes that take place in the street, where poor manufacturers and operatives are to be found in dozens, with their hand carts, hawking about from shop to shop their week's work in search of a purchaser. And the prices which they are obliged to sell at is something astonishing—prices which, in several cases, does not pay for the materials and labour, without allowing anything for profit. From twelve to sixteen, and even eighteen hours a day is often worked by cabinet and chair makers, who make furniture articles on spec for Curtain Road.'

These poor 'operatives', known as garret-masters, were the lowest form of furniture manufacturers in Victorian times. Some idea of the acute misery of their life can be gained by reading a description of it in *London Labour and the London Poor* (1861), by the philanthropist, Henry Mayhew.

The garret-master, as the name implied, worked in a garret on his own account for other craftsmen. In the 18th century the garret-master was paid at piece-work rates for articles or parts of articles commissioned by a master craftsman; the same practices existed in other trades such as watch and clock makers, jewellers and silversmiths. A natural pride and trade loyalty prevented the important master from squeezing the rates of the garret-master. The garret-master had no capital and in ordinary circumstances had to live a hand-to-mouth existence selling one batch of goods before he could purchase materials to start on the next. In the 19th century furniture was no longer directly commissioned by the masters and the garret-master was forced to hawk his wares round the streets in a hand cart from one shop to another. He was desperate to sell because generally his active capital was tied up in his work; this the purchaser well knew and did not fail to take advantage of it.

This was the darkest side to the production of Victorian furniture, and the goods produced by the garret-masters must have been the standard type in working class homes. Most of this furniture, one suspects, has long since fallen to pieces.

CHAPTER TWO

Furniture Styles up to 1867

IT IS convenient that the turn of the century can reasonably be taken as marking a very real change from the light and graceful traditions of the late 18th-century 'classical' taste to a far heavier and more ornamental style. With few exceptions, weight and ornament were to become the keynotes of the 19th century.

The very early 19th-century designers were still largely dominated by their own version of classical ideals, as may be seen from the design books. The general term favoured at this date was 'Grecian', but the interpretation differs from earlier standards. Also a wider interest in history and archaeology had brought in many exotic elements such as Egyptian and Assyrian. Piranesi and indeed Adam had foreshadowed this movement. Within a very few years from the opening of the century, as we shall show, other popular historical and intellectual interests had begun to have a wide effect on design, and the sources of inspiration ranged from Mediaeval and Renaissance to 'all the Louises'.

Craftsmen living in a traditional age have always felt the need of ornament to give to an article a pleasing appearance. In the 18th century all kinds of wares both costly and cheap—a silver teapot, a brass tobacco box or a country chair—had their functional design relieved by some form of decoration, be it engraving, chasing, carving or turning. From Gothic times tradition told the craftsman how to be restrained in the use of ornament and how ornament should be contrasted with a plain surface which acted as a foil. He avoided over-elaboration, for there was no necessity to invent ornament or devise decoration, because it was already at hand, being part and parcel of the current style.

It cannot be pretended that in the 18th century the use of ornament was always impeccable. For example, the individually delightful Chinese and Gothic styles, popular in the mid-18th century, cannot be said to blend happily together on one piece; this unfortunate combination took place and can most often be seen on mirror frames. However, traditional guidance saved most 18th-century furniture from over-ornamentation and gave it much of its artistic quality.

When the traditional neo-classic style began to decline at the close of the 18th century, and the mixed architectural Grecian and Egyptian styles came in, considerable changes took place in English furniture design. A comparison between Sheraton's designs in his *Drawing Book* (Fig. 2) and George Smith's *Household Furniture* (Fig. 3) clearly shows this.

The tendency during the first quarter of the 19th century was for the structure of furniture to become heavier and for carving and turning to become coarser; this was especially noticeable

28

in tables, chairs and sofa frames. The trend is also noticeable in mouldings decorating book cases, wardrobes, sideboards and writing tables.

This gradual evolution can best be realised by the comparison of drawings in contemporary design books. The four sideboards illustrated in Figs. 2–5 are taken from design books by Thomas Sheraton, George Smith and T. King.

Another element present in the furniture of the first quarter of the 19th century was the urge to create new designs which would tempt customers by their unusual and exotic nature. Cabinet and chair makers sought inspiration from designs of furniture depicted on Greek vases and marble reliefs. The Greek chair, with carved legs and back, was copied and became the standard dining chair of the Regency period. The excavations at Herculaneum and Pompeii also brought to light actual examples in bronze or marble of tables, chairs, couches and tripod stands. The table with three animal legs, each of which was surmounted by a lion head, originated from this period. This motif of a lion-headed leg became extremely popular, being used also in the form of trusses to ornament book cases, sofas and armchairs.

The sphinx head was another favourite motif and was used to decorate chairs, tables and book cases. Other Egyptian motifs employed by the furniture trade were the figure of Isis, the winged sun disc, birds, Sphinx heads, hieroglyphics and crocodiles. These motifs were culled from current archaeological and design books of the time, such as Baron Denon's *Voyage dans la Basse et Haute Egypte* (1804) and Percier and Fontaine's *Recueil de Décoration Intérieure* (1801).

This new outlook on furniture design brought about by the quest for novelty shows that tradition—so strong a guiding force in the 18th century—was waning well before 1837.

As already described, the craftsman in a traditional age was his own designer. This changed in the early 19th century, for design was no longer a part of the craftsman's work, because it now came into the hands of draughtsmen and ornamentists.

At the moment when furniture was made without the guidance of a traditional style, but with designs invented on a drawing board, it can be said that furniture making changed from a craft to an industry.

The furniture designers followed the path laid down by the architects who were producing designs for houses in a number of past styles. An early Victorian architect, in describing architectural design, divided it into two principal classes—the Classical and the Picturesque:

> 'The Classical character . . . is that of stately, symmetrical, refined balance and repose with simple, elaborate elegance in the ornament: the Picturesque character that of unsymmetrical, vigorous, sparkling piquancy with the ornament not so much refined as animated.'

The Grecian style popular in the early days of the century still remained in favour in the 1830s and 1840s. It was considered the modern style and was the one specially favoured by the furniture trade. Of the Picturesque styles there were two that were much used by the architectural profession as well as by the furniture makers—Mediaeval or Gothic and Elizabethan. Another style that was extremely popular for decoration and furniture was the French Rococo or Louis XV style. (The Louis XIV style was often referred to in error as having rococo ornament.) Examples of decoration in the French Rococo style are preserved at Windsor and Belvoir Castles.

All these styles had come in before Queen Victoria's reign, for they are mentioned in J. C.

Loudon's comprehensive treatise, *Encyclopaedia of Cottage, Farm and Villa Architecture*, the first edition of which appeared in 1833. 'The principal styles of design', he wrote, 'as at present executed in Britain may be reduced to four, viz., the Grecian or modern style which is by far the most prevalent; the Gothic or Perpendicular style, which imitates the lines and angles of the Tudor Gothic architecture; the Elizabethan style, which combined the Gothic with the Roman or Italian manner; and the style of the age of Louis XIV, or the florid Italian, which is characterised by curved lines and excess of curvilinear ornaments.'

The publication of such books as Joseph Nash's *Mansions of England in the Old Time* and the popularity of Sir Walter Scott's romances, which appeared between 1814 and 1832, led many people to develop a sentimental yearning for the picturesque past. It was not, however, the outlook of the antiquary, but the Victorian businessman's way of escape from the industrial environment of his everyday life. The pastiche of an Elizabethan room, with its oak panelling, stained glass windows and carved oak cupboards, tables and chairs was a not uncommon treatment in many Victorian well-to-do homes.

Besides Loudon's *Encyclopaedia* there were other contemporary books which confirm the fashion in the 1830s and 1840s for furniture and decoration in the Elizabethan style. *Furniture with Candelabra and Decoration*, by R. Bridgens, 1838, has designs in the Grecian, Elizabethan and Gothic styles. Those, however, in the Grecian taste display a more assured handling by Bridgens than his efforts to make a modern sideboard, a table or a cabinet look picturesque by the application of Elizabethan strap and arabesque work and caryatides.

The Victorians were vague about the application of the description 'Elizabethan'; this was especially the case with regard to chairs, which, although they certainly included some of the decoration associated with this period, were more often than not in a style which was not current until the reign of Charles II some seventy years later. An example of this application of the term 'Elizabethan' to chairs in a late-Caroline style can be seen in Figs. 17 and 108. Occasionally the Victorians were correct in their use of the description 'Elizabethan style'; an example of this can be seen in the mid-Victorian folding armchair illustrated in Fig. 11.

In 1840 the firm of H. W. and A. Arrowsmith, 'Decorators to Her Majesty', produced *The House Decorator and Painter's Guide*. This book illustrates a number of 'Elizabethan' interiors (Fig. 6). Some have the walls with oak panelling copied from Elizabethan wainscot, while others are 'an adaptation of the Elizabethan ornament to a modern apartment'. An interesting comment by the authors on Elizabethan decoration is that 'it has of late become very fashionable, and chiefly from the circumstance that it has required the use of the antique carved furniture which, although so much admired, was before altogether useless or out of place'.

Interest in old oak furniture was a natural sequence to the 19th-century revival of Elizabethan architecture and decoration. At this period old furniture was seldom valued from the collector's point of view, as it is today, but because it was picturesque and curious. There was considerable destruction of oak furniture of the 16th and 17th centuries, which was sawn up and mutilated for its carved parts; these parts were then reconstructed to form modern furniture, such as sideboards, buffets and cupboards, that were utilitarian as well as picturesque in the Victorian home (Fig. 12). Loudon's *Encyclopaedia* gives a description of this trade, which must have accounted for large quantities of chests, bedsteads, press-cupboards and panelled rooms of the Elizabethan and Jacobean periods:

'We have now upholsterers in London who collect, both in foreign countries and in England, whatever they can find of curious and ancient furniture, including fragments of fittings-up of rooms, altars and religious houses; and re-arrange these curious specimens, and adapt them to modern usage. . . . Whoever in the present time [1833] wishes to furnish and fit up a house in such a manner as to produce a new and strange effect on the spectator, cannot attain his end at less expense than by having recourse to Elizabethan fragments. . . . Wilkinson of Oxford Street and Hanson of John Street have extensive collections of Elizabethan and Dutch furniture and carvings, from which a judicious compiler of exteriors might clothe skeleton frames so as to produce objects of curiosity and interest at a very trifling expense.'

The Victorian version of furniture in the Gothic style was recognisable by the ornament only; for the structure of chairs, tables, book cases and sideboards, upon which the tracery, crockets, pinnacles, buttresses and other Gothic motives were applied, was the same structure as used for furniture in the Grecian and Elizabethan styles. Loudon gives in his *Encyclopaedia* an account of 'Gothic Furniture for Villas'. 'What passes for Gothic furniture', he writes, 'among cabinet-makers and upholsterers is, generally, a very different thing from the correct Gothic designs supplied by Architects who have imbued their minds with this style of art.'

He becomes enthusiastic about 'a Drawing Room fitted up and finished in the Gothic style' (Fig. 7). 'We need not express an opinion of this interior; for every reader, we think, must be pleased with it. Even the studies of furniture which it affords are interesting; the Gothic piano-forte and music-stool with the Canterbury on the left hand and the music-stand on the right; the Gothic couch with its footstool; the two beautiful chairs; and, finally, the firescreen, all claim attention and are each separately worthy of study.' Every age, including our own, has its Loudons and only the verdict of years can determine whether they are right or wrong.

The French Rococo style of Louis XV was very much used by the decorating and furniture trades in the 1830s and 1840s. In the *House Decorator* there are numerous plates showing the wall and chimney-piece treatment with applied Rococo panels reaching from the skirting to the cornice (Fig. 8).

In an account of a room described as in the Louis XIV style (Louis XV in fact), the authors write that 'the popularity of this style may be in a great measure traced to the anxiety for French furniture, which the wealthy in the country have for some time past evinced'.

Loudon does not approve of the French style because of the great expense of carrying out the designs and 'because we think a style distinguished more by its gorgeous gilding and elaborate carving than by anything else, unsuitable to the present advancing state of public taste'.

The *House Decorator*, besides showing designs of rooms in Elizabethan, French and Gothic styles, also has illustrations of other styles of decoration 'as used by the architects of the present period'—Roman, Arabesque, Pompeian, Cinque-Cento and François Premier.

The writer on furniture and decoration of the 1830s and 1840s made a point of listing the various current styles which were described and illustrated in his book, thus disclosing the eclectic character of design of this early Victorian period.

Henry Whitaker, in his *House Furnishing, Decorating and Embellishing Assistant* (1847), informs his readers on the title page that his book consists of 'original designs in the Grecian, Italian,

Renaissance, Louis XIV, Gothic, Tudor and Elizabethan styles'. It was written to encourage improvement in the designs of manufacturers. 'The cultivation of the industrial arts,' the author writes, 'in connection with design, must therefore be important to the public at large as well as to the manufacturer. It is still more important to attend to the beauty as well as the utility of productions, when the superiority of our continental neighbours in taste, not only baffles us in neutral markets, but is said to claim a preference even on our own soil.'

The author also suggests that the manufacturer should be encouraged, or rather compelled, to keep a designer. 'Expect not a tradesman to be a designer', he writes, 'any more than you would expect the driver of a locomotive to be an engineer or a stonemason an architect. . . .'

Whitaker's designs consist mainly of furniture, but also include chimney-pieces, grates, stoves, iron railings and window curtains. After the lapse of a hundred years, it is easy to see that they are only elaborate versions of typical Victorian design. The furniture is over-loaded with ornament culled from various styles, and the structure upon which the ornament has been applied bears no relation to the style. As an example of this, there are illustrations of two writing tables which are the same in shape and design of structure; it is only in their ornament that they differ, for one is in the 'Elizabethan' style, and the other in the 'Renaissance' (Fig. 13). The employment of a different style of ornament to decorate the same structure was a popular trick of the Victorian designer. That it was common at the time is evident from what is written in *The Cabinet-Maker's Assistant*:

> 'Everyone connected with cabinet-making is aware of the difficulty of obtaining good and novel Designs of Furniture. When, however, such designs are obtained, everyone is equally aware how comparatively easy it is to adapt them to the kind of work required; they may, in fact, be multiplied indefinitely by engrafting the decorations of one on the forms of another, and in many ways that will suggest themselves to every practical man.'

The designs and writing of Henry Whitaker serve to illustrate how artists, architects or designers help to create the age in which they live, and consequently share the same outlook. Some have more artistic discernment and a greater insight than others, but these qualities seldom free them from the sentiments of their own time. Living as we do in a later age, we find it less easy to agree with this author when he wrote that 'the intention of the present work is to furnish designs which, when placed in juxtaposition with ordinary productions of similar articles, will show purchasers that "beauty may be obtained as cheaply as ugliness", and that the former while equally useful is surely more ornamental. This truth will be at once manifest to those who attend to the simplicity of the designs, and the accurate drawing of the patterns'.

This statement sums up the average Victorian concept of beauty, which it equates with 'ornamental' value. Whitaker's idea in designing furniture was to ring the changes on the use of ornament, which he applied to tables, chairs, sofas, chiffoniers, book cases and bedsteads; the structure of this furniture, however, was based on designs that were common to all the furniture trade. He valued ornament above everything and he did not think that the form of furniture and its proportions were the essentials that endowed furniture with good design.

This view of the function of ornament by the Victorians was summed up by Ralph Wornum in his prize-winning essay, *The Exhibition as a Lesson in Taste*, when he wrote: 'Ornament is not a luxury but, in a certain stage of the mind, an absolute necessity.' This attitude differed from that of the craftsman of the 18th century, who looked upon ornament as a means of pleasing enrichment and believed that in itself it was not essential to good design. By covering and at some periods almost smothering furniture with carving, most Victorians felt that they were imparting an artistic quality to it. It was generally thought that the more the ornament, the more the piece of furniture possessed beauty. This outlook is also to be found reflected in silver, metalwork, jewellery and chinaware of the period. A plain surface was an anathema to them. Many 18th-century panelled rooms were canvassed over so that their nakedness could be hidden under an elaborate wall-paper.

The English were not the only nation with this love for ornament. Matthew Digby Wyatt, in an article about the Great Exhibition in the *Journal of Design*, wrote: 'All European nations at the present time begin manufacture with ornament and put utility in the background.'

The design of the structure of Victorian furniture changed only periodically. Twenty-five or more years had to elapse before there was any marked difference in the basic forms of sideboards, tables and sofas.

It was easy to apply ornament on to a surface, but to alter the structural forms of furniture, which people had been accustomed to and which in most cases had been derived from functional requirements of the time, was a far more radical change. A change of this nature was seldom the product of one mind, but the combined effort of many.

One of the difficulties of dating the styles of Victorian furniture is that a number were current at the same time. It is comparatively easy to determine—from design books, contemporary writing and exhibition catalogues—when a style first came into fashion. Unlike the 18th century, however, the advent of a new style did not necessarily mean the decline of an old one, and several styles would remain fashionable at the same time. Some manufacturers and shops would prefer one particular style and would make a speciality of it and continue it after others had changed to something different. In comparison, the dating of 18th-century furniture, with its orderly progression from one style to the next, is a simple matter.

The best signposts are the various International Exhibitions, two of the most important of which were held in London—the Great Exhibition in 1851 and the International Exhibition of 1862. In Paris, the three most outstanding were those of 1855, 1867 and 1878.

English furniture makers of standing exhibited in Paris in the same way that their continental rivals did in London. It is the catalogues and their illustrations, and the reports and criticisms of the furniture at these exhibitions, that disclose to the student the trend of design during these three decades.

A number of the reviews or editorial comments on the Great Exhibition reveal there was no sense of complacency about the state of contemporary design. Even before the Great Exhibition, the *Journal of Design* of 1849 had some caustic comments on the so-called 'taste' obtaining at the time:

'All the art of the present day is typical of the prevailing eclecticism. There is no general agreement in principles of taste; what principles may happen to be recognised seem only transitional—transitional to what? No one can say. Everyone conceits himself to be pope in taste and infallible in knowledge of art; he is his own absolute *arbiter elegantiarum*. Everyone selects his own style of art, and the choice usually rests on the shallowest individualism. Some few take refuge in a liking for "pure Greek", and are rigidly classical; others find safety in the "antique"; others believe only in Pugin; and some extol the Renaissance. We all agree only in being wretched imitators.'

Richard Redgrave, artist, Royal Academician and authority on industrial design, makes a number of pertinent remarks concerning ornament. He wrote in the *Supplementary Report on the Exhibition of 1851* that 'novelty was one of the sources of bad taste in modern ornament'. To this statement he adds: 'Now, however, our efforts are of an entirely different nature, and the hunger after novelty is quite insatiable; heaven and earth are racked for novel inventions, and happy is the man who lights upon something, however *outré*, that shall strike the vulgar mind, and obtain the run of the season.'

He lays down the principle that 'Design' has reference to the construction of any work both for use and beauty, and therefore includes its ornament, but he adds that 'Ornament' is merely the decoration of a thing constructed. He goes on to say that the tendency of the present time is to reverse this rule, and give to ornament the principal place and that many of the exhibits of the Great Exhibition show that utility and construction are made subordinate to decoration. He points out that designers think of ornament before construction and therefore they 'construct ornament rather than ornament construction'. Redgrave condemns 'a new species of ornament', which he says is of the most objectionable kind. He calls it 'merely imitative style', in which 'ormulu stems and leaves bear porcelain flowers painted to imitate nature, and candles are made to rise out of tulips and china asters, while gas jets gush forth from opal arums'.

He also comments on how ornament is multiplied by the machine or the mould and that the manufacturer should accordingly realise his responsibility in seeing that the design of the prototype should be a work of beauty and that everything should be done and no expense spared in the employment of skilled designers and artists to make it so. The following remarks are revealing:

'In this country artists are paid little better than workmen, and a belief seems to prevail that knowledge, skill and taste come by nature: the artist has often no interest in the result of his labours, his name is unknown, his pay is niggardly, and what there may be of beauty and excellence in his work is often spoiled by the alterations of the manufacturer, who makes no scruple of setting his own taste above that of the artist, and altering and changing a design at his sole pleasure.'

The review goes on to say:

'We design and execute in every conceivable style. We imitate every extant school. We are equally at home in the reproduction of classical and Byzantine art—Etruscan ware and Majolica: we can execute Chinese or Athenian with the same facility; we can forge—perhaps that is the most appropriate term—an Egyptian obelisk or a Corinthian capital, a so-called Gothic moulding, or a Sèvres cup ... Ours is an age of transition; we are in the midst of the breaking up of the great deep of the past, and we are perhaps struggling after a wider and more distinct range of truth. But ours is certainly a chaotic period. The Exhibition shows that we are most skilful mimics, that we know how to reproduce classics—that we can restore everything. But what do we create?'

34

Redgrave in 1851 expresses much of the feeling that was later to inspire William Morris and his followers. His criticisms show that England was by no means devoid of people with artistic sensibility. It is not always appreciated that the low state of English industrial art was fully realised by some, well before the Morris movement.

There is an interesting similarity between Redgrave in the 1850s and Morris some fifteen years later in that they both failed to realise that it was essential to come to terms with machinery. Redgrave in his *Supplementary Report on the Exhibition of 1851* levels some harsh and often well-deserved criticism at the exhibits, but he fails to make any suggestion about how necessary it was that any improvement in design would have to accord with machine production.

Redgrave dealt with the problem of the advent of machinery by simply not discussing it. Morris on the other hand dismissed machinery by saying that its use was entirely bad. He fostered a return to hand-craftsmanship and by so doing, as we shall show later, he was defeating his own object.

In the official catalogue of the 1851 Exhibition the furniture exhibits are described as Elizabethan, Tudor, Gothic, Louis XIV, Renaissance, Italian, Arabian and Old English Illuminated style. The illustrations of furniture depict examples all heavily enriched with carving. The designers adopted the modern forms of sideboards, chiffoniers, bedsteads and wardrobes, and applied to their surfaces the ornament of the various past styles. In many cases there are several styles of ornament all present on one piece. In other cases the furniture has been so heavily enriched that the ornament has distorted the form. All the bedsteads in the illustrations are of the same type—a double bed with a half tester (Fig. 14). However, the variations of design, caused by the liberal application of ornament on the bottom, head-boards and cornice of the tester, has given each bed an entirely different character. A view of part of the Furniture Court at the Crystal Palace is illustrated (Fig. 9).

A sideboard table and wine cooler by Gillow of London, although called in the *Art Journal Illustrated Catalogue* 'of bold design and spirited execution', shows a medley of ill-assorted ornament (Fig. 10). The table top, which is serpentine in shape, is supported at each of the two front corners by an eagle with outspread wings. This design was inspired by the carved wood and gilt examples which were fashionable in the time of George II. Gillow's eagles, even allowing for the drawing, have a vulture-like expression and are standing precariously on slabs of stone. To add to the weakness of the design, a shaped frame richly carved with rococo scrolls holding a looking-glass plate is fixed to the back.

The furniture sent to the Exhibition by provincial makers in most cases shows the greatest elaboration coupled with an incongruous mingling of motifs and a strange use of scale. A typical example is a walnut and ebony carved cabinet by Freeman of Norwich, which displays cupids with outspread wings, bearded male heads, female caryatides and dragons. The mixed proportions of the design can be realised by comparing the difference in scale of the small caryatides, the large male heads and the even larger heads of the dragons (Fig. 15).

A study of the work of the Warwickshire school of carving throws additional light on Victorian thought and taste in the 1850s. Warwick had become and was to remain throughout the Victorian period an important centre for fine and elaborate carving. Two of the leading firms were Cookes (who in later years became Collier and Plucknett) and Kendalls of Chapel Street, who continued at the same address until 1919. Thomas Kendall, the founder of the firm, had served his apprenticeship under the master carver, J. M. Willcox, and it was while he was in his last year of apprenticeship that they worked together on a sideboard commissioned by the County of Warwickshire as a present to Queen Victoria in 1857. Unfortunately they forgot to ask the Queen if she would accept the piece and when it was offered she refused it. Mrs Lucy then bought the sideboard for £2000 for Charlecote Park (Figs. 16 and 17). It is recorded in the Kendall family papers that John Ruskin, after contemplating the piece for some time, turned to Mrs Lucy and said: 'It is indeed worthy of Michelangelo'.

Cookes had produced the Kenilworth buffet, which is an essay in the picturesque and a *tour de force* of the Warwickshire school of carving (Figs. 18–20). The panels are executed in relief, portraying scenes from Sir Walter Scott's novel, *Kenilworth*. The centre panel shows Queen Elizabeth entering Kenilworth Castle (Fig. 19), the left one her meeting with Amy Robsart and the right her interview with Lord Leicester. The buffet, which is of oak, is today at Warwick Castle and is alleged to have been made from one great oak tree in the castle grounds.

This buffet is a typical example of the importance the Victorians attached to sentiment. A picture or piece of sculpture made additional appeal because of the idea portrayed by the subject. It was for this reason that many Victorian pictures tell a story, and in the case of the Kenilworth buffet this narrative element is extended to a piece of furniture.

Another of the Cookes' sideboards of the same design, but with the more general theme of the chase, is illustrated in Figs. 21 and 22. This example is more typical of the production of the Warwickshire school, for even in the 1850s and 1860s vast pictorial and historical sideboards must have been something of a speciality. Both Kendalls and Cookes not only produced these great sideboards, but supplied, particularly to the local nobility, all articles of household furniture. Even with such pieces as firescreens, loo tables, mirrors and chairs, the carving and turning were intricate and elaborate; this can be seen by studying some original drawings of Thomas Kendall (Figs. 23–28).

The Warwickshire school, although the best known, was not alone in producing this elaborate carved pictorial furniture. A piece known as the Chevy Chase sideboard (Fig. 29) closely resembles the work of the Warwickshire school and is conceived on the same sentimental and pictorial lines as the Kenilworth buffet. It is, however, the work of Gerrard Robinson (1834–1891), of Newcastle. This sideboard is inspired, as the name implies, by the ballad of Chevy Chase, which tells the story of Harry Hotspur, the son and heir of the first Earl of Northumberland, in his fight with the Earl of Douglas. Harry Hotspur was determined to go poaching in the territory of Lord Douglas and this scene of the hunt is elaborately portrayed in the lower central panel. Lord Douglas arrived at the hunt and a great battle ensued; this is the subject of the top central panel. The four smaller panels show other aspects of the story in elaborate detail (Figs. 30 and 31).

It is believed that the sideboard was commissioned by the fourth Duke of Northumberland for the dining room at Alnwick; this would seem highly probable as it is just the sort of piece, romantically depicting his ancestors, that a Victorian nobleman in the 1860s would delight in owning. The history of the sideboard is known, however, from the time it was made (1857–1863) and although it may have been commissioned by the Duke, it never came into his possession. Today it is at the Grosvenor Hotel in Shaftesbury.

That Gerrard Robinson was a carver in the very first flight can be seen by looking at the illustration of his Chevy Chase sideboard. Two other sideboards, one telling the story of Robinson Crusoe and the other with a Shakespearean theme, are among known examples of his work.

The work of these furniture carvers, although produced in the provinces and not under any direct metropolitan influence, caused considerable comment both at the Great Exhibition and in the years following.

The few French exhibits illustrated in the 1851 Exhibition catalogue show, in comparison with the English, a far greater understanding and taste in the use of ornament, although they err on the side of over-elaboration. A French designer was not often guilty of mixing his styles, for he realised the importance of keeping all his ornament in harmony.

On the other hand, most of the illustrated English pieces endorse Matthew Digby Wyatt's remark that the manufacture began with ornament and that utility was relegated to the background.

The International Exhibition of 1855 held in Paris is of importance to our study of Victorian styles, for it shows the change of design that had taken place in English furniture since the Great Exhibition. This change was undoubtedly due to the French exhibits at the latter, which revealed the undoubted superiority of the French, both in design and craftsmanship. In fact, so much was this the case that several English firms now employed French designers. The effect of this was quickly marked, for in the 1855 Exhibition some of the English exhibits showed a purer style and a more sure use of ornament than the French.

For instance, one of Jackson and Graham's pieces in the 1855 Exhibition was a cabinet in the Louis XVI style, designed by the firm's chief designer, Eugène Prignot, who had been with them for the previous six years. Not only did Jackson and Graham employ a French designer for their cabinet, but four other foreign craftsmen as well—Carrier, who modelled the caryatides; Claudio Colombo, who carved the figures from the models; Protat, another modeller who executed the figures on the top of the glass frame; and Phoenix, who did nearly all the flowers and ornaments.

This information is recorded in Digby Wyatt's *Report on the Furniture of the 1855 Paris Exhibition*, in which he says that 'it is a subject for congratulation that these foreigners should be working for us'. The report also mentions by name other designers who were employed by English firms of the period; among them was Professor Semper, who designed a cabinet exhibited by Holland & Sons.

Digby Wyatt praises the work produced by old-fashioned firms. 'Unquestionably much excellent work has been got up by some of the older firms, such as Seddons, Morant, Snell, Crace, Taprell, Holland and Gillow, whose establishments have had the benefit of the artistic talent of men such as Fossey, Beaugard, Depeux, Ash, Turner, Mulholland, Whitaker, Dyer, etc.'

He goes on to say that such firms as Jackson and Graham, Trollope, Holland and Levien show a great improvement on their productions since 1851, but in some of the others he regrets 'the evidence of a still lingering propensity of the sarcophagus style, in which the quantity of the wood rather than the quality of its treatment, seems to be regarded as the test of merit'. He adds that it would be unjust to deny the English credit for the use of excellent materials and perfect workmanship, but that they are limited in their use of woods, 'neglecting to a great extent variety and contrast of colour and texture in the different parts of a piece of furniture'.

He also regrets the English furniture makers' conservatism in their failure to use ebony, tortoiseshell, bronze or brass fittings as well as carry out the more elaborate processes of fine carving, mosaic, marquetry, buhl, etched metal and engraving; also veneering on swept and curved circular surfaces and many other intricate processes which, he remarks, 'seem to be excluded almost *in toto* from the catalogue of English capabilities'. He considers also the advantages possessed by the French workmen in their free libraries, museums and other institutions where they could educate themselves and improve their taste. And he has this advice to give to the Government of the day:

> 'If we would elevate the English workman we must recognise some other stimulant to his energies than beer; we must provide museums for him, where, as at Marlborough House, he may see what others have done before him, and better than him in his own trade: we must get some free libraries, where he may be able to go and improve himself; we must put some better and more ideal monuments than we already have into our public streets, spending more money upon their art, and less upon the quantity of materials of which they are made; we must, in short, educate his eye, and through his eye, his mind, by giving him access to the best models of fine and industrial art.'

It was still thought at this date that individual master craftsmen could influence design as they had done in the 18th century. It was not yet fully understood that the arrival of machinery, and the vast growth in the country's wealth, and consequently in demand, were forces which no traditional training, however good, could effectively control.

A study of the exhibits both at the 1855 and 1862 Exhibitions shows that the most important French firms vied with each other in producing the highest quality craftsmanship in the form of furniture that suited modern requirements, but yet was based on the historical styles of the past. They aspired to make their modern furniture works of art, for their ambition was to rival the achievements of the great *maître ébénistes*, who worked in the hundred years before the Revolution.

Such furniture was not a servile copy, but had elegance of design combined with faultless execution. When, in fact, a French cabinet-maker did make an exact copy of a piece of old furniture, it was so perfect that only the expert could distinguish it from the original. This reproduction French furniture of the middle decades of the 19th century was costly, and Lord Hertford paid 90,000 francs for the copy of the famous *Bureau du Roi Louis XV*, which is today in the Wallace Collection. The original of this piece is at Versailles, but the superb quality of the copy made by Pierre Dasson can be only partly realised from the illustration (Fig. 32).

When this magnificent copy was made, the marquetry was carefully treated to match the faded condition of the original; over the years the marquetry on the copy has faded more than on the original so the difference is now considerable. However, this painstaking attention to detail was typical of the thoroughness of the French in all aspects of furniture making in the 19th century.

Theirs was an entirely different viewpoint from that of today, when copies of old furniture, however well executed, are considered to be of little account, for having been made outside the period they must of necessity lack the spirit which inspired the original work.

Furniture Styles up to 1867

The appreciation and decorative value of 19th-century French furniture often caused wealthy Englishmen to buy it in preference to that of their own country. This was one of the reasons that made the best English firms seek to emulate the French both in design and quality of craftsmanship.

Although the mahogany flat-topped desk illustrated in Fig. 33 is now in England, it is almost certain that the designer would have been a Frenchman. Its elegance of design is typical of the French or French-designed exhibits at the Exhibitions in London of 1862 and in Paris of 1867.

Besides the contemporary French furniture, old French furniture made before the Revolution was also bought by rich Englishmen like Lord Hertford. This furniture today often poses a difficult problem, for to make the furniture more acceptable to the Victorian purchaser the old ormulu mounts were often removed and new and more elaborate ones applied. Today these substitute mounts are about a century old and it makes them difficult to detect as later additions and they are often credited with being 18th-century originals.

The influence of French design was particularly marked in the production of London firms of the first rank such as Jackson and Graham and Holland & Sons.

There is no doubt that the International Exhibitions, taking place at short intervals of five to eight years, had a great influence on English furniture making. When the exhibits of the English manufacturer were seen side by side with the French products, even the least critical could not fail to realise the gap which separated them, both in terms of design and of craftsmanship. In making the English furniture makers design-conscious, these Exhibitions undoubtedly served a most useful purpose.

That in 1862 there was still considerable room for improvement is evidenced by the recommendations of the Jury of the International Exhibition held in London in that year. In the foreword to the section on Furniture and Upholstery, they make the following pertinent criticisms:

'In all the objects exhibited, which Art has contributed to adorn, it is easy to perceive that invention has little share, and that their principal merit consists purely in an exact imitation of some well-known original. Sometimes strange attempts at novelty have been made by mixing together details belonging to different styles, and thus isolating the laws of harmony . . .'

The Jury then recommended that exhibitors should commission eminent artists—'fully apprised of the peculiar conditions of the manufacture of household furniture'—to help them over matters of design.

To judge from the lavish three-volume work by J. B. Waring, *Masterpiece of Industrial Art and Sculpture*, the general trend of furniture design at the Exhibition seems to have been towards the historical styles, particularly of 18th-century France (Fig. 34). Designs inspired by the Gothic style of the Middle Ages provide the next most important influence (Fig. 35).

The Elizabethan style, so prominent a feature of the 1840s, now declined as the Mediaeval style appeared to take its place. Augustus Welby Pugin (1812–1852), architect and mediaevalist, who was commissioned under the direction of Sir Charles Barry to design the Gothic ornament of the Houses of Parliament, exerted an important influence in this Gothic revival as it applied to furniture.

Digby Wyatt, in his report on the 1855 Exhibition, sums up contemporary feeling about the death of Pugin:

'Thus there can be no doubt that this groping after the light of the past revealed to that great man, whose loss the world as well as his friends must deplore, the late A. W. Pugin, those sensible principles of structure and ornament which, as applied to furniture, have given to some of our leading cabinet-makers, such as Mr Crace, the power to revive the best characteristics of the middle ages, without demanding any servility in reproduction.'

John G. Crace met Welby Pugin during the time his firm were carrying out the painted decoration of the interior of the Houses of Parliament. At the Exhibition of 1851 Crace, in conjunction with Pugin, was responsible for the decoration of the Mediaeval Court, which was one of the outstanding features at the Crystal Palace. The exhibits in the Mediaeval Court included an oak cabinet in the Gothic style, designed by Pugin and made in Crace's workshops (Fig. 36).

Crace himself was an ardent mediaevalist, and in 1857 he read a paper to the Royal Institute of British Architects, in which he maintained that the Gothic style was eminently 'suitable to a nobleman's house of the present day' and that it was capable of being as graceful, light and elegant as any other style.

He was greatly influenced in his mediaevalism by Pugin, who designed furniture for his firm. Designs for three tables and a corridor bench are illustrated in Fig. 37; they are of interest because they are signed by Pugin and bear the stamp of John G. Crace & Son, 38, Wigmore Street. The table illustrated in Fig. 38, which was made by Crace's firm, may well have been inspired by the one (top left) shown in the drawing. The detail and decoration in the drawings are suggested only by the slightest lines and Pugin seems to have been content to leave the interpretation of them to Crace.

This library table was made for Mr Watts of Abney Hall, Cheshire, as also was the book case illustrated in Fig. 39. This book case has a certain similarity to the cabinet that Pugin designed for the Mediaeval Court (Fig. 36).

Among the papers of the Crace family there is an account of the history of the firm, which was of the first importance in all aspects of interior decoration throughout the 19th century. The following extract written by J. D. Crace (the son of Pugin's friend) gives some idea of the size of the firm and the diversity of the work which they undertook:

'The business was carried on from father to son from 1745 till 1899. I joined in 1854 when my father and grandfather were both actively engaged in it. At that time many large works were in progress, including portions of the Houses of Parliament, and numerous mansions in all parts of England and in Ireland. Among other large works in the succeeding five years were the Fine Arts Exhibition at Manchester, where alone some hundred or more men were employed, at the Crystal Palace, the Town Hall at Leeds [which was redecorated by us some thirty or more years later], the S.S. *Great Eastern*, and many others.

'The number of men employed was very variable—probably from one hundred to two hundred at one time—except in the winter. In the succeeding years, the works included many London Clubs and the Halls of City Guilds, besides public and private mansions in London, the Provinces, Scotland and Ireland.'

It is interesting to note today that J. D. Crace gave the following as one of his reasons for winding up the firm in 1899: 'The harassing anxiety attached to the employment of men particularly by Trades Union action, and finally by the Employers' Liability Acts.'

Another mediaevalist and a newcomer to the furniture trade was William Morris. His firm, Morris, Marshall, Faulkner & Co., was founded in 1861 and received their first success by gaining a medal for their furniture at the 1862 Exhibition. However, as we shall show in the next chapter, the interest of Morris and his associates for the mediaeval was in many ways different from that of Crace and Pugin.

With the more up-to-date members of the furniture trade, the Grecian style, which had lasted throughout the first half of the 19th century, rapidly went out of fashion after the Great Exhibition. However, as with nearly all other Victorian styles, the Grecian was continued in the provinces considerably longer. When the Grecian style was dead in England, the French turned again for inspiration to the Classic world, and a revival of these designs was to be seen not only in their furniture, but in their metalwork and jewellery. Even in England there were some firms which took their cue so closely from Paris that they had already noticed the trend of advanced French design, and in the 1862 Exhibition J. H. Levien and Howard & Sons showed furniture in the Pompeian style (Figs. 40 and 41).

The illustrations in Waring's book reveal quite clearly that a number of the French exhibits were of such high quality in their execution as to come within the category of works of art. One ebony cabinet, the work of the eminent cabinet-maker, Barbedienne, elaborately ornamented with bronze in a finish that gave the appearance of oxydised silver, certainly comes in this class judged by the standard of the time.

Another example of a work of art, as far as fine craftsmanship and elaborate use of rich material was concerned, was a carved cabinet by the firm of Fourdinois of Paris. This closely followed the traditional design of a French cabinet of the 16th century. Unlike such a cabinet, however, it had encrustations of lapis-lazuli, bloodstone and jasper, and there was an inlay of ivory with silver masks, delicately chased (Fig. 42). Every care had been taken to make the cabinet an incomparable example of modern French craftsmanship. This piece was sold to an Englishman for £1,400.

It is interesting to compare the difference in thought and taste that wholeheartedly approved Fourdinois's cabinet in 1862, but eleven years earlier considered the Kenilworth buffet one of the most admirable works at the Great Exhibition.

A sidelight on the times is provided by Waring's remark on the subject of foreign labour in England. The revolutions in France of 1848 and 1851, he states, had driven many French craftsmen and artisans to England, and again in 1862 'the troublous state of Europe' had led to a greater number of foreign workmen—French, Italian and German—being engaged in the furniture trade in England than at any known time.

The English furniture trade had received a similar infusion of new blood from France some 150 years before this time when the Edict of Nantes was repealed and Huguenot craftsmen fled to this country. Then they were prominent in all branches of the furniture trade, but most particularly as gilders. England, indeed, had always had an attraction for foreign craftsmen because of her more stable working conditions and greater prosperity than most of her continental neighbours.

The four men employed by Jackson and Graham on the modelling and carving of the cabinet which they sent to the 1855 Paris Exhibition were not untypical of the type of craftsmen and artisans who were now adding their talents to the English furniture trade. Not all of them were under steady contract to one firm, for a number remained free-lance; Lamb of Manchester employed on the modelling of their 1862 Exhibition cabinet a certain H. Protat, who had been one of Jackson and Graham's foreign workmen in 1855.

Another important factor affecting English cabinet work at this period, which is noted by Waring in his description of the furniture at the 1862 Exhibition, is the number of English furniture-makers who were employing architects to prepare designs for their exhibits. It would, therefore, seem that the best English firms were now making every effort to emulate the 'works of art' of the French.

In the preamble to the furniture section of the catalogue of the Paris Exhibition of 1867, the importance of employing 'distinguished artists' in all the trades connected with furniture and decoration is emphasised, for this 'co-operation has introduced art and good taste into the manufacture'. This is not without interest for it shows that the French and the English were both confronted with the same problems and were following the same line of thought as to their solution.

Unfortunately, there are few reviews of this Exhibition and therefore it does not greatly help us in following the trend of English furniture design. The only evidence of value is that provided in the *Reports of Artisans*. The Society of Arts had made it possible for a number of skilled English artisans to visit Paris, so that each of them could report on the exhibits which he saw in his trade, and on the French methods of work and manufacture. Unfortunately, these reports were written by craftsmen who were more interested in production than design. The report on cabinet-making contains one pertinent remark—that 'our British exhibitors have a preference for satinwood and gold; it looks very rich and chaste. In the French department ebony is all the rage, whole suites of bedroom furniture black entire, but richly carved'.

An unusual bedroom suite made by Dyer and Watts, of Northampton Street, was of pine, stained and grained to imitate satinwood. The writer's comment is: 'I should judge this to be the finest specimen of stained wood, as it quite deceives the eye, and is well finished.' A pine wardrobe by this firm, stained and painted to represent maplewood decorated with inlay, is illustrated in Fig. 44.

Jackson and Graham, unlike the other English exhibitors with their preference for satinwood and gold, followed the French taste in the use of ebony. In another report on cabinet work, the writer says of the exhibits of Jackson and Graham: 'The palm for workmanship must be given to Messrs Jackson and Graham of London, whose exhibit is the finest in the entire Exhibition: an ebony cabinet, richly inlaid with ivory, lapis lazuli, and excellently engraved, being the principal production.' This firm displayed a very similar cabinet at the International Exhibition of 1871 (Fig. 43).

Wright and Mansfield exhibited a large satinwood cabinet in the neo-classic taste with gilt mouldings (Fig. 45). This cabinet is today in the Victoria and Albert Museum, having been purchased by the Government direct from the Paris Exhibition for the then considerable sum of £800. Wedgwood plaques, which decorate the door panels of this piece, were also used by J. R. & W. Hunter, who showed a wardrobe and toilet table decorated in this manner.

This Wright and Mansfield cabinet caused considerable interest at the Exhibition and it is not unreasonable to suppose that it encouraged the use of plaques for decoration in the general furniture trade. A small good quality drawing room cabinet with corner display cupboards, made about 1865 and incorporating small plaques, is illustrated in Figs. 46 and 47.

The *Reports of Artisans* goes on to mention that 'although the French contribute the best-designed cabinet-work to the Exhibition, it will be noticed that it is very much alike, and contains the same kind of ornament [the French Renaissance] and general treatment, one as another. Black being, as it were, quite the fashion, much of this is ebonised and thus spoilt'.

The report on chairs by Benjamin Lucraft, a chair-maker, is depressing as far as those of English manufacture is concerned:

'The next and last section is the British; and, without the least doubt or hesitation, yet with the most profound regret, I say it, our defeat is as ignominious, and, I fear, disastrous as it is possible to conceive. We have not only made no progress since 1862, but it seems to me we have retrograded. The English chairs and sofas do not at all compare with the French in elegance, and are by no means superior in make.'

If the styles of the Victorian era are divided into two periods, the 1867 Exhibition makes a convenient division. Until this date nearly all the various styles in furniture had sprung from the trade itself. Although the better firms had employed architects and designers, they were very much within the trade and had none of the prestige and influence which designers were to gain towards the end of the 1860s. Pugin and William Morris might be considered to be an exception to this. Pugin's influence, however, on the general furniture trade was strictly limited, although Morris's firm was being favourably noticed by the general public as early as the 1862 Exhibition, which was only one year after the foundation of the firm.

The period from the accession of the Queen until 1867 can be sub-divided into two periods taking the Great Exhibition of 1851 as the dividing line. There is no doubt that all that is worst in Victorian furniture design was exemplified by the exhibits at the Crystal Palace. Unfortunately, today these pieces are the best known and still thought to be most typical of all Victorian furniture.

In the period up to the Great Exhibition there were so many styles, and such a frantic search for novelty, that it is neither possible to discern any logical progress from one style to another, nor to determine the influence or importance of any particular designer or manufacturer. For this reason the dating of furniture made at this time is harder than in the rest of the reign and cannot be done with any certainty except where documentary evidence exists for an individual piece.

In spite of the mixture of styles, there are in this period two noticeable characteristics. The first was the use of new and unusual materials. The technical advances that were made at this time meant that there were many new materials available such as carton-pierre, gutta percha and papier mâché. Furniture was also made from bone, leather and iron, those made from iron being more often than not painted to simulate wood. There was also a chair made of coal (Fig. 54), but even the Victorians considered this to be more for show than use. Of all these new materials, perhaps papier mâché was the only one that was an attractive and suitable material for furniture, being ideally suited to small and decorative pieces; it is discussed in more detail in Chapter 5.

The second characteristic was the great value placed on rich and flamboyant carving. This love of carving was responsible for the great success of the Warwickshire school of carving, which we have already discussed. The work of the Warwickshire carvers was exceedingly costly handwork and could be afforded only by the wealthy. In the general mind, carving still meant expense and being able to afford a highly carved piece gave an air of affluence to the owner. The fact that the majority of the carving on the standard productions of the furniture trade was no longer done by hand, and was now carried out by new methods at a small percentage of the former cost, did not reduce its attraction.

When condemning the furniture shown at the Crystal Palace in 1851, it is important to remember that it was not entirely typical of the furniture trade as a whole. This can be said to some lesser extent about all 19th-century exhibition furniture. The manufacturers were well aware that novelty and technical skill intrigued the Victorian public above almost everything else and they were at pains that their own exhibits should display those qualities to a greater extent than their competitors. Thus a headlong race developed; the result was that firms tended to display their most costly, most elaborate, most vulgar but least typical pieces. These pieces were designed to attract as purchasers, kings, noblemen, governments, museums and immensely wealthy people and it was not intended that the ordinary middle-class householder should do anything but observe and wonder.

During the period between the Great Exhibition of 1851 and the Paris Exhibition of 1867 furniture design rapidly improved, mainly due to the French influence. The majority of furniture now had some uniform style and although there were still differences, certain main characteristics could be observed. Lines were straighter and simpler and the better-class furniture producers moved away from the Rococo. Carving was still enormously popular but there were some quite discernible changes; the carved portions tended now to be contained in panels and did not wander indiscriminately over the entire piece. The outlines of the furniture had a more architectural form, which showed quite clearly and was not blurred by the carving.

Carved figures were now considered almost essential on all important pieces; these figures tended to become larger than formerly and were a dominating feature. The increase in the size of the figures and the change in the application of carving can be seen by comparing the Alscot and Kenilworth sideboards (Figs. 22 and 18) with the two pieces, one by James Lamb of Manchester (Fig. 48) and the other by Jackson and Graham (Fig. 49). The sideboard by Lamb was exhibited at the 1862 Exhibition.

Besides the large, carved figures, great mirrors were typical of this period, which can also be seen from Figs. 48 and 49. Great strides had been made in the technique of producing looking glass and the Victorians, who could not resist any opportunity to show off their technical skill and ability, incorporated vast mirrors in the superstructure of their sideboards.

This particular style was not really recognised or named by writers at the time, but apart from Crace & Son and a few others who supported the Gothic, it was very popular with the trade. Besides this un-named and somewhat indefinable style, the English cabinet-makers were copying the past and adapting the styles of the 18th century with a preference for the neo-classic of Robert Adam and the French style of Louis XVI.

CHAPTER THREE

Furniture Styles
after 1867

IN THE middle of the 1860s a new style started to gain popularity: it was known as the 'Early English' or 'Modern English Gothic'. It was described as the 'most sincere and simple' of all styles. Crace & Son and a few others had been producing furniture in this manner from the time of the Great Exhibition, but the majority of the furniture manufacturers and the general public had not been deeply influenced or interested. Interest in the 'Early English' style was roused by the publication of a book which had a wide circulation both here and in America entitled *Hints on Household Taste*, by Charles Lock Eastlake (1836–1906), the nephew of Sir Charles Eastlake, the painter who became President of the Royal Academy. This book was published in 1868. The chief characteristic of the 'Early English' style which it propounded was the method of construction, based on that of joined mediaeval woodwork; it produced massive furniture held together by pegged joints without the use of glue.

Although the author illustrates his book with his own designs (Figs. 50 and 51) and some pieces of furniture are described as 'executed from a design by Charles L. Eastlake', it has not so far been possible to trace any examples of this furniture. In America the furniture trade produced a debased Gothic style, which was far removed from Eastlake's ideas. However, such was the influence of his book that furniture produced in this manner became known as the 'Eastlake style'.

William Morris, with his love of craftsmanship, was an adherent of the 'Early English' style. His firm Morris, Marshall, Faulkner & Co. (founded in 1861 and reorganised in 1865 as Morris & Co.) were supporting this style some years before the rest of the furniture trade. It was the simple direct method of construction that appealed to William Morris. Unlike Crace and Pugin, who produced Gothic furniture because they considered it to be the ideal *design*, Morris supported it because he considered it to be the ideal *construction* and typical of all that was best in handcraftsmanship. He was without Pugin's almost spiritual attachment to the Gothic, and the following lines from his *Lesser Arts of Life* show that his admiration and support came from what seemed to him more practical reasons:

'Our furniture should be good citizen's furniture, solid and well made in workmanship, and in design should have nothing about it that is not easily defensible, no monstrosities or extravagances, not even of beauty, lest we weary of it. As to matters of construction, it should not have to depend on the special skill of a very picked workman, or the super-excellence of his glue, but be made on the proper principles of the art of joinery: also I think that, except for very movable things like chairs, it should not be so very light as to be nearly imponderable; it should be made of timber rather than walking-sticks.'

Morris goes on to write about 'workaday' furniture, which should not only be well made and well proportioned but simple to the last degree. He also adds ' . . . if it were rough I should like it the better, not the worse'.

In spite of his writings and the production of his firm, Morris personally had little interest in furniture and apart from one or two pieces for his house, he never appears to have designed any. The chief furniture designer of his firm was the architect Philip Webb (1831–1915), who was associated with Morris from the foundation of the firm. He designed a large number of country houses and also produced designs for metalwork, jewellery and fabrics.

The massiveness of his joined furniture is clearly shown by the two tables illustrated in Figs. 55 and 56. Webb also designed pieces in a different version of the 'Early English' style. These pieces were constructed on vaguely Gothic lines, but the principal object was to provide large, plain areas which could be decorated by painters. Several such pieces were produced by Morris, Marshall, Faulkner & Co. and shown at the 1862 Exhibition. They must really be judged by the quality of their painting rather than by the design of their structure. A wardrobe, which now belongs to the Ashmolean Museum (Fig. 52), was designed by Webb and painted in 1859 by Edward Burne-Jones with scenes from Chaucer's 'The Prioress's Tale' as a wedding present for Morris. A cabinet illustrated in Fig. 53 was also designed by Webb and painted by Burne-Jones and was one of the exhibits at the Exhibition in 1862.

It is easy to see the difference between this interpretation of the 'Modern English Gothic' and the earlier one of Crace and Pugin, which produced their elaborate, highly finished exhibition pieces. Pugin, in fact, designed a considerable amount of simple furniture for the houses he built; this furniture was designed in a plain, unelaborate Gothic manner. However, it was never shown at Exhibitions, nor were the designs published, so its influence on the furniture trade was negligible. The public considered the furniture designed for the House of Commons and the Mediaeval Court typical of his work.

Bruce Talbert was another exponent of the 'Early English' style. He was an architect and professional designer specialising in furniture and decoration. He trained in Glasgow and after spending three years in Manchester as a furniture designer, moved to London in 1865. He quickly became an established and influential designer and published *Gothic Forms Applied to Furniture* in 1867 and *Examples of Ancient and Modern Furniture* in 1876. Jackson and Graham, Collinson and Locke and Holland & Sons were among a number of firms for whom he designed.

An interesting piece designed by him and made by Holland is illustrated in Figs. 58 and 59. This piece, which displays all the characteristics of Talbert's style, is illustrated (Fig. 60) in his *Gothic Forms Applied to Furniture*. In the introduction to this book Talbert describes the Gothic technique of furniture making and how he dislikes cabinet work. 'In these old works', he writes, 'the wood is solid, the construction honestly shewn, and fastened by tenons, pegs, iron clamps, nails, &c.; it is to the use of glue that we are indebted for the false construction modern work indulges in; the glue leads to veneering and veneering to polish.'

His dislike for veneer made him suggest that where it was impossible to use finely-grained woods in the solid, such woods should be inserted in small panels as ornaments, thereby leaving the construction parts of plainer wood with 'dead surfaces'. This would allow the plain parts to give contrast and value to the whole.

There are several drawings of interiors in his *Gothic Forms Applied to Furniture* and the one illustrated in Fig. 61 gives a clear idea of the style of his furniture and of the whole effect he was trying to create in a house. A further example of his work is illustrated in Fig. 57.

This love of Gothic construction resulted in his furniture, like that of Philip Webb, being bulky and heavy, although he lightened it by panels and Gothic tracery. In the Paris Exhibition of 1867 Holland & Sons exhibited a sideboard by Talbert. Criticism of this sideboard by the artisan who was sent by the Society of Arts to review the Exhibition is of interest, for it showed how this heavy, joined furniture was looked upon by a craftsman who thought of furniture in terms of the cabinet-maker's craft. His summing-up of the sideboard was that it was 'a piece of dining room furniture that I cannot admire, as it looks too heavy, and more like a piece of rough joiners' work than a fine piece of cabinet-work, which we expect to see in a gentleman's house; it appears too ecclesiastical for household furniture; allowance must be made, however, for this kind of work being seldom got up'.

The last sentence is interesting; this contemporary comment bears out the fact that exhibition pieces were by no means considered the prototypes for the furniture to be produced over the next few years.

A noticeable feature of both Talbert's and Eastlake's furniture is that the backs of sideboards and book cases are formed of narrow-width boards, sometimes set vertically and sometimes at 45 degrees. This construction was an affectation of the Gothic, the furniture of which style was made of boards of irregular width; but they were not all of a standard width as in this Victorian furniture, where the boards were uniform because of their machine production.

A designer of the period and a pioneer of the 'Early English' style was Richard Charles, who first makes his appearance in 1860 with the publication of the *Cabinet Makers' Monthly Journal of Design*. Charles was well aware of the defects of English furniture design, as is made clear in his foreword to the first issue when, referring to the Exhibition of 1851, he says: 'The few [pieces of furniture] produced in England that claimed their share of merit, emanated principally from Foreigners in this country.' He attributes this to the fact that 'there is not that order established amongst us which is indispensable, as the legitimate basis of success; but rather a kind of disorder which we can better understand than describe'.

Charles's own style seems to have anticipated that of Eastlake and Talbert. A book of designs by him (probably made originally for his *Journal of Design*) contains sixty-one lithograph coloured plates (Figs. 62–66); some of the examples, with their simple joined and plank construction and their carved medallions, bear a marked resemblance to the work of his better-known contemporaries, Eastlake and Talbert. One of the plates is dated 1867, the year in which Bruce Talbert's first book of designs was published and a year before Eastlake's *Hints on Household Taste*.

Many motifs of Gothic design are displayed in Charles's work—panels filled with boards; the edges of rails and stiles chamfered and shaped; and the backs of sideboards and testers of beds crenellated. Some of the most important pieces have panels carved with roundels, but, in general, the pieces, although resembling in their treatment Talbert's and Eastlake's work, differ in one respect—which is that the furniture follows in its basic design the contemporary furniture of the time.

The sideboards are of the pedestal type with looking glass backs, the chiffoniers are typical mid-19th-century shape, so too are the pedestal dressing tables with mirrors, and the washstands with tiled backs. The beds illustrated are, with the exception of one four-poster, all half-testers. Also included in the designs are Davenport desks, bedside cupboards, towel rails, dining room buffets, carved curtain cornices, piano stools, work and occasional tables, and screens; to all of which he has given the same 'Early English' character.

The reason that he employed the standard designs of contemporary furniture was undoubtedly to give to his pieces a utilitarian value so that they should meet public demand. '*The Journal*,' he writes, 'will contain a large number of Designs, which will be found to combine the ornamental with the practical, as well as copies of ancient and modern master-pieces . . .'

The great interest in Charles's designs lies in the fact that we find here evidence of a little-known pioneer of the 'Early English' style; for which pioneering work some of his better-known contemporaries have up to now received all the praise.

A noticeable characteristic of this 'Early English' school was the rectangular form of the structure, for seldom had a piece of furniture any curved or shaped lines. It followed the craft of the mediaeval joiner, which demanded a framework of posts and rails held together by mortice-and-tenon joints. Curved members meant cutting wood to waste and therefore they were seldom present in traditional joined furniture. On the other hand, the chief characteristic of Victorian trade furniture was for chairs and couches to have rounded backs and arms and cabriole legs; for sideboards and tables to have shaped fronts; for door panels to have rounded tops and for the mirrors at the backs of sideboards to be shaped and curved. Seldom was this trade furniture of rectangular form, for the love of richness and curved outline was the chief standby of the trade designer.

Eastlake in his *Hints on Household Taste* condemns such furniture because of its curves, and he says that if the choice is left to ordinary upholsterers nothing but vulgar furniture would result. 'The tendency of the present age of upholstery is to run into curves. Chairs are invariably curved in such a manner as to ensure the greatest amount of ugliness with the least possible comfort.' Eastlake also condemns the backs of sideboards and the legs of cabinets, which are weakened by their curved design, and as for drawing room tables, he writes they are 'curved in every direction' (For illustrations of these remarks, see Figs. 67–70, of tables, chairs, couches and sideboards from a City furniture maker's catalogue, *circa* 1865).

Eastlake, like Morris, had a grave objection to french polishing, for he says that 'the surface of wood thus lacquered can never change its colour or acquire its rich hue which is one of the charms of old cabinet-work'. Eastlake also remarks that furniture 'should be in strict conformity with modern requirements, to ignore which would be sheer affectation'. He mentions 'Art Furniture' and says that the chief drawback to its popularity with people of ordinary means is its cost. Elsewhere, he writes that 'the true principles of good design are universally applicable; and if they are worth anything, can be brought to bear on all sorts and conditions of manufacture'. This sound statement, however, is not always borne out by some of his own furniture designs which he illustrates; for a number of the pieces, although showing straightforward joinery in their construction, have been unnecessarily elaborated in order to achieve a picturesque effect.

The term 'Art Furniture', as used by Eastlake, shows quite clearly that by the late 1860s a distinction was being made between the standard products of the furniture 'warehouse' and the furniture made by a firm who retained artists and architects such as Webb, Talbert and Eastlake to design for them—thereby giving their furniture an 'Art' quality. For the first time we find such expressions as 'Art Furniture', 'Art Decoration' and 'Art Wallpapers'. In fact, the word was in current use in the 1870s and 1880s among authors of books on furnishing and decoration as well as furniture manufacturers who, immediately the term 'Art Furniture' became accepted, adopted it to boost their own products.

Reference must be made here to an architect who designed furniture, William Burges (1827–1881). His furniture was particularly mannered: it was Gothic in character and decorated in polychrome. Burges's chief patron was the third Marquess of Bute, for whom he rebuilt Cardiff Castle (1865) and Castell Coch (1875), which was almost a complete ruin before he was commissioned to restore it.

The decoration and furniture for Castell Coch were of a fanciful character. In Lady Bute's bedroom the furniture was decorated 'in gold, red and blue with touches of pink, pale green and white'. The large fitted wash-stand (Fig. 71), so much in the style of Burges, was not, however, designed by him but by John S. Chapple in 1891 (ten years after Burges's death). A Gothic wash-stand designed by Burges is illustrated in Fig. 72. The folding doors below the basin are pierced like the doors of a 16th-century aumbry. An aumbry was a food cupboard and the piercing was a necessary part of the design for it ventilated the interior. One can only speculate why this wash-stand cupboard should require ventilation—also such massive strap hinges to hold such light doors.

This highly colourful and exotic interpretation of Gothic by Burges had little effect upon Victorian furniture, for he rarely designed pieces other than for his clients or his own house. However, like Philip Webb, Burges designed one or two comparatively plain pieces which left large smooth surfaces to be decorated by artists; there is a book case in this manner decorated by no fewer than eleven well-known artists, also a plain cabinet painted under his direction by E. H. Poynter, which depicts the battle between wine and beer.

It was from the 1870s onwards that furniture styles grew more complex; new influences and new professional designers were now at work. The effect of this was that Talbert's and Eastlake's 'Early English' style declined and from the solid, joined construction of mediaeval times the pendulum swung to a lighter and more fanciful style. One temptation which these designers resisted was that they did not use curved and shaped forms, but adhered to the straight, structural lines of the earlier school.

This cannot be said, however, of the main body of the trade, as furniture design still revelled in the curved and complicated shapes of French Rococo. Even when the trade copied good work, as they seldom failed to do directly it became current, they modified it according to their own ideas, thinking that by adaptation or additions it would become more saleable; their products were often a bizarre version of the original.

The change which took place after Eastlake's and Talbert's 'Early English' style had declined is thought to have been partly due to T. E. Collcutt, the architect for the Imperial Institute.

His style was by no means a complete break-away from that of Eastlake and Talbert; he continued to avoid curves and his painted panels have a connection with his predecessors. Collcutt did away, however, with the unpolished and heavy look of the early furniture, which he replaced with a finished quality more associated with cabinet-work than joinery. This can be seen by the design of the cabinet (Fig. 73) made in 1871, with its small panels decorated with painted designs.

The corner shelves in both the upper and lower parts were a new feature at this date. Once this fashion for small corner shelves and recesses for *bric-à-brac* came in, the furniture trade used such features *ad nauseam*. They were used not only for drawing room cabinets, but also for overmantels, and even chimney-pieces had recesses and small angle shelves.

Eastlake would appear to have been one of the first designers to have thought of the overmantel with shelves, for he illustrates in his book a chimney piece the shelf of which is surmounted by what he calls 'mantelpiece shelves' (Fig. 51).

Collcutt designed the cabinet illustrated for Collinson and Locke, a firm of cabinet-makers and decorators. They brought out a catalogue of furniture designs in 1872, most of the furniture in which appeared to have been designed by Collcutt (Fig. 76). This catalogue ensured that the designs were soon copied by the furniture trade; the refinement of Collcutt's work, however, went unrecognised and in the hands of the trade his furniture soon became hackneyed and debased.

Galleries with turned spindles now became popular with furniture makers, not only for the tops of cabinets and the shelves of overmantels, but also fitted to a shelf fixed above the door of a room on which plates and vases were displayed. These galleries were a feature of design that was copied from the French, who were fond of using them to prevent china from falling off cabinets and tables; even the tops of upright pianos and canopies of beds had galleries.

That this 'Early English' style was in its last phase is evident from a letter published in 1873 in the *Furniture Gazette*. 'We have had a surfeit of "Early English" lately, with its everlasting turned balusters, bits of bevelled glass, art tiles and the rest. I know', the writer adds, 'it is rank heresy to say a word against the *soi-disant* "art furniture".'

With the 'Early English' style becoming debased and no longer fashionable, an important new influence on design made its appearance. This was the Japanese style. Until the middle of the 19th century, Japan had been a virtually closed country, which permitted neither trade nor travellers. In the early sixties, with the opening of the country, Japanese goods in the form of prints, pottery and lacquer ware began to make their appearance in English shops. With this new trade arising between the two countries a vogue for things Japanese resulted. Victorians, with their avid desire for something new, seized upon the art of Japan to influence their design, as earlier they had used Greece and Egypt.

Christopher Dresser, who started work as a Lecturer in Botany, was to become one of the most prolific and best-known professional designers of his day. He produced designs for many different materials, including metalwork, glass, pottery, textiles and a certain amount of furniture, although there are not enough known examples of the latter to make a considered judgment on his contribution in this field. He designed in very many different styles, but he was, above all, an exponent in the art of Japan. He visited that country in 1876. In 1880 Dresser was both Art Editor of the *Furniture Gazette* and founder of the 'Art Furniture Alliance'. The multitude of his designs in the Japanese manner and his writings, which contain high praise for the art of that country, helped to stimulate the general public's fast rising interest in all things Japanese. Two examples of his furniture are illustrated in Figs. 74 and 75.

In 1862 the International Exhibition was held in London and it was here that the first collection of Japanese decorative art was shown. William Burges reviewed this Exhibition in the *Gentleman's Magazine* (July, 1862) and made special mention of the exhibits in the Japanese Court. Being a mediaevalist, he appreciated the true mediaeval character of Japan's contribution and made distinction between it and the modern mediaeval work in England. This was at the best a laboured copy, whereas the Japanese displayed in their ivory carvings, bronzes and armour, all the real character of mediaeval design and handiwork. In fact, he summed up the Japanese Court as being the real mediaeval court of the Exhibition.

This enthusiastic wave for things Japanese swept the country and many collections of Japanese bronzes, lacquer ware and prints were formed. In due course the Japanese influence extended to the decorative arts, in which it left its imprint on the design of pottery, porcelain, wallpapers, textiles and cast iron ware. The style also became popular among furniture manufacturers, who produced 'Anglo-Japanese' furniture which had very little, if any, Japanese characteristics in it because the real merits of the style were not understood by them.

This did not apply, however, to Edward William Godwin, who was one of the first people to take an interest in Japanese decorative art and to design furniture inspired by this style. He was a distinguished architect whose eclectic taste ranged from Italian Gothic to modern Queen Anne. He was a friend of both Oscar Wilde and James McNeill Whistler. For Whistler he designed the White House in Tite Street; it was of a plain, functional design unlike any other house of the time. As a furniture designer, Godwin, unlike his friend William Burges, did not care for 'Early English' style. He became fascinated by Japanese art and took to designing furniture inspired by that country.

As early as 1862, the year of the Exhibition, he decorated his house in Bristol with plain colours; he used simple old furniture and hung Japanese prints on the walls. He devoted much of his time within the next ten years to the study of Japanese art and it was remarked of some wallpaper patterns designed by him that 'Mr Godwin had gone beyond most people's notions of the boundaries of civilisation and has added Japan'.

A piece of furniture designed by Godwin is illustrated in Fig. 78. It has the merit of simplicity and displays strong Japanese characteristics, although far from being anything like the furniture used in Japan. Two further examples of his work are illustrated in Fig. 79. In 1877, William Watt of Grafton Street published a catalogue in which the designs were by Godwin. The first page of this catalogue is illustrated in Fig. 77. From this can be seen the way that Godwin's mind was working. Two further pages from this catalogue are illustrated in Figs. 124 and 209. Godwin was not guilty of applying Japanese ornament to a piece of Victorian furniture in order to make it 'Japanese', in the way that the hack designers of the furniture trade found it so easy to do.

By 1880 Max Beerbohm in an essay could write of the aesthetes 'hurling their mahogany into the streets'. In the same year *Punch* was full of drawings depicting the aesthetes, usually set against a background of spindly furniture and Japanese prints, and by 1881 Gilbert and Sullivan's opera *Patience* had taken the whole Aesthetic Movement for its target. Godwin's friend Whistler became strongly influenced for a time by Japanese art.

Jackson and Graham were among the more important furniture manufacturers who adapted Japanese designs, and two pieces made by them in this style are illustrated in a contemporary book, *The Decoration and Furniture of Town Houses* (1881), by the well-known architect of his day, Sir Robert W. Edis. From the description which Edis gives of the cabinet (Fig. 80) it would appear that the panels were of lacquer or painted decoration. Although, by illustrating these examples, Edis clearly approved of furniture in the Japanese style when it was made by a firm such as Jackson and Graham, he had a number of reservations to make when the style was used by the hack designers of the furniture trade. 'We must have care', he writes, 'that so-called "art decoration" does not degenerate into the feeble prettiness of ignorant designers or into the fashion of so-called "art papers".' He goes on to condemn 'flimsy' furniture imitated or copied from Japan which has no element of real culture or imagination.

In an account of 'Japanese Furniture' which appeared in the *Furniture Gazette* of November 11th, 1876, the editor described how the growing taste for Japanese art was becoming manifest in the furniture trade. At the warehouse of Crawley, Morris & Co. at 64, City Road, there was a collection of 'elegant' drawing room furniture made of Japanese bamboo. This bamboo furniture consisted of all sorts of tables, what-nots, hall lamps, jardinières and even beds. *The Cabinet Maker and Art Furnisher* also writes about 'novelties and new inventions' in bamboo and illustrates an umbrella stand shown in Fig. 81.

This bamboo furniture was sold at a very moderate price owing to the cheapness of the material, which also had the advantage of strength, for there was no fear of breakage even in 'articles of a delicate nature'. There must have been a number of other makers who specialised in bamboo furniture judging by the amount which is extant today. Bamboo was also used by the leading furniture makers in conjunction with other woods; a desk by Howard & Sons of Berners Street is illustrated in Fig. 82. The legs are bamboo, but the superstructure is of satinwood and the result is a light and pleasing piece.

A new style of architecture known as Queen Anne came in during this crowded period. It affected interior decoration as well as furniture. The architect, J. J. Stevenson, was one of the initiators of the style and his paper read to the Architects' Conference in 1874 on 'The Recent Reaction of Taste in English Architecture' was one of the first occasions when the style was mentioned. 'The style', he said, 'in all its forms has the mark of truthfulness; it is the outcome of modern wants picturesquely expressed.' The architect, Professor Robert Kerr, was another keen supporter of the Queen Anne style, the modern adaptation of which he described to Lord Palmerston as the 'Modern European Style'.

The Queen Anne style house, built of red brick with small pane sash windows and a roof with numerous gables, quickly became fashionable and at the same time a revival of furniture 'after Chippendale' took place. While the sale-room prices recorded the new enthusiasm of collectors for the old pieces, a more widespread demand was satisfied by not 'too slavish' copies of this master cabinet-maker's furniture. *The Furniture Gazette* of June, 1873, reflects this new vogue when it prints the first of a series of designs taken from Chippendale's *Director*, 'for which', the editor writes, 'there is now a great demand'.

In 1878 in her book, *The Art of Beauty*, Mrs H. R. Haweis wrote of the 'recent rage for "Chippendale" and so-called "Queen Anne" furniture'. She continued by saying that Chippendale's furniture was not beautiful in the artistic sense, but only in a technical one. 'The heavy lyre-backed chairs with horse-hair seats, the fragile tables which seem to aim at having *no* legs, the straight diamond-paned book cases of mahogany, with brazen-handled drawers—useful they may all be in their way—beautiful they never can be called.' Mrs Haweis accounts for the interest taken in Chippendale furniture to be the 'natural reaction' against the modern vulgar taste in furniture to which cultivated people had been for so long accustomed.

In the 1870s and 1880s, following upon the success of Eastlake's *Hints on Household Taste*, a number of other writers entered the battle against the poor design of the day. Apart from Edis and Mrs Haweis, such writers as W. J. Loftie, R. A. Garrett, Lady Barker and Mrs Orrinsmith were all agreed on one thing—the badness of contemporary 'trade' furniture. W. J. Loftie was convinced that, for those who could afford it, the solution lay in collecting antiques and the masterpieces of the past.

On the other hand, Mrs Orrinsmith, with a view to the limited means of her middle-class readers, was in favour of modern adaptations of the best 18th-century designs. In this she agrees with Edis who, in one of his Cantor lectures to the Society of Arts in 1880, wrote of the 'exquisitely beautiful satinwood furniture of Adam's style exhibited at Paris by Messrs Gillow . . . an example of exceedingly delicate and graceful adaptation of 18th-century design to modern furniture; the panels of the various pieces formed in walnut-wood with ebony inlaid, and laid over with box-wood, carved down, so as to show the ebony behind in exquisite cameo-like medallions after Flaxman; the delicate enrichments and ornamentation of gilt lacquer-like character were all elegant in design and marvellously beautiful in workmanship'.

These enrichments of inlay, cameo-carving and gilt lacquer were additions intended to make the traditional designs of the furniture richer and more decorative. Firms like Gillow's and Holland & Sons, who specialised in making furniture inspired by the 18th-century designs, were also fond of decorating the panels of their sideboards and writing tables, often made in satinwood, with neo-classic urns and swags of satinwood inlaid in contrasting woods (Fig. 83). The edges of drawers and tops of sideboards and chests were also decorated with satinwood bandings.

Edis in his *Decoration and Furniture of Town Houses* illustrates three pieces in the neo-classic style (Fig. 83), all made by Holland & Sons. This firm illustrated in their catalogue (Fig. 84) a drawing room that they had completed for a customer. They simply called the style 'eighteenth century' and wrote: 'This period is very frequently adopted in the arrangement of the drawing room or Boudoir, where lightness combined with elegance are sought for. Decorated or inlaid satinwood is frequently used successfully in this period.'

The making of fine quality reproductions of 18th-century furniture was continued in varying degrees throughout the whole of the 19th century; in the 1870s, however, it was exceedingly popular. These high quality copies made in the last thirty-five years of the Victorian era have in many cases acquired fine patination and at first sight they would deceive the expert. Such an example is illustrated in Fig. 85 and only on closer inspection can its date be detected by the method of construction. This chair leaves no doubt as to its origins, for apart from the construction it is labelled (Fig. 86) with the name of Howard & Sons, Ltd., of Berners Street, London, who were prominent Victorian furniture makers.

Hepplewhite, Sheraton and Adam designs were now widely copied in addition to those of Chippendale. Also both English and French cabinet-makers were fond of enriching plain pieces of old furniture in order to make them more ornamental and therefore more saleable. *The Pall Mall Gazette* (1875) writes on this subject:

'Throughout the last century every piece of furniture, however common, was made in the same style and on the same general design as what is now known as "decorative" furniture, and there are still great quantities of it to be bought at a lower price than the same goods could be made for. These common chairs or tables or cabinets only need the addition of appropriate ornament and exhibition in a fashionable dealer's rooms to take rank and value as fine old Chippendale or marquetry furniture. There are many workmen in London who are mainly or wholly employed in "enriching" goods for the old furniture market. The common oblong mahogany table that used to be found in every bedroom has an openwork "gallery" added to its top and a veneering of fretwork glued round its edge. The useful mahogany sideboard which once existed in every "parlour" has bands and medallions of satinwood judiciously inserted. The chairs or the cabinet which passes into the hands of the inlayer as a piece of unadorned mahogany or walnut comes out of them glowing in all the colours that nature or the dyer can give to woods. The vendor probably tells his customers but the truth. He says that the furniture is old; and so it is. There is nothing new about it except the bits of decoration here and there, which do not make up a hundredth part of its bulk, though they increase its price twentyfold.'

Like the earlier French pieces, that had new mounts applied to them in the Victorian period, these plain 18th-century English pieces went through somewhat the same process; instead of the application of ormolu mounts and floral marquetry, they were enriched by bands and medallions of satinwood and by edgings of cross-banded veneer. Again, like the French, many English pieces which received this treatment a hundred years ago are highly deceptive and their decoration has often passed as original.

As the century advanced the movement which William Morris had initiated as early as 1861, and to which he had tried to give a lead by the products of his firm, crystallised into what came to be known as the 'Arts and Crafts Movement'.

Although the ideals of Morris inspired and influenced this movement, much of the furniture that was produced was far removed from the simple Gothic-style furniture of Morris's designer, Philip Webb. The Arts and Crafts Movement is still the subject of research and study and can only be outlined here.

The movement consisted of various groups and associations of craftsmen and artists. The Century Guild, founded in 1882 by A. H. Mackmurdo and Selwyn Image, was a typical association. An example of Mackmurdo work is illustrated in Fig. 87. The Art Workers' Guild (1883), the Guild of Handicraft (1888) and Kenton & Company were others.

As would be expected from these associations of gifted and individual designers, many different trends developed. The work produced by the movement, however, was the only important influence on furniture design in the last fifteen years of the Victorian period.

With the formation in 1888 of the Arts and Crafts Exhibition Society, the general public became familiar with the movement's aims and products; an exhibition was held in the year this Society was founded and succeeding exhibitions in 1889, 1890, 1893, 1896 and 1899. Although individual members of the movement were developing their own personal and strongly individual styles, it was not possible to design or work in entire isolation. The frequency of the exhibitions and the innumerable articles, essays and works produced by the members of the movement on all aspects of design made this impossible. The Century Guild had its own magazine, *The Hobby Horse*, and there were many other publications which helped to unite the movement and establish its aims.

William Morris, writing the preface to a book entitled *The Arts and Crafts Essays*, published in 1893, outlines the aims of the Society as follows:

> 'Our art is the work of a small minority composed of educated persons, fully conscious of their aim of producing beauty, and distinguished from the great body of workmen by the possession of that aim. . . . It is this conscious cultivation of art and the attempt to interest the public in it which the Arts and Crafts Exhibition Society has set itself to help, by calling special attention to that really most important side of art, the decoration of utilities by furnishing them with genuine artistic finish in place of trade finish.'

The problem of endowing furniture with good design was more difficult than with any other of the crafts. What the members of the Arts and Crafts Society did not realise was that, unless the manufacture of furniture was on an economic basis, all efforts towards universal good design would be of no avail. In the last quarter of the 19th century the production of furniture had to be on a considerable scale in order to meet the large demands of a population of about twenty-five millions. Handcraftsmanship, which the Society considered so essential a feature of good design in furniture, could not produce a sufficient volume of goods at a cheap enough price for so large a public demand. Woodworking machines, which had been invented in the Victorian era, increased production and reduced cost.

The problem of good design in furniture could not, therefore, be solved in the way that the Arts and Crafts Society hoped. They were right in that they employed 'educated persons'—artists and architects—to design furniture, but quite wrong to insist that this furniture was to be hand made and therefore the design influenced by the requirements of traditional handcraftsmanship. The members of the movement did not realise that hand-made furniture belonged to a past England with a population of five millions. Unless furniture could be produced to suit the vastly changed conditions, it could have no significance, either artistic or economic, because the great majority to whom Morris and his friends wanted to sell would be unable to buy because of the small amount produced and the correspondingly high cost.

Much of the furniture displayed in the Arts and Crafts Exhibitions was expensive; it was often decorated with marquetry, gesso or applied metalwork. The very people whom Morris most despised—the rich 'Philistine' businessmen—were almost the only ones who could afford the individually designed, hand-made products of the new movement.

As the ugliness of contemporary furniture coincided with the use of machinery, it is not surprising that this late Victorian generation of artists and architects condemned machines. They felt that the machines were responsible for the lack of quality in furniture, in that they made poor copies of what formerly had been made better by hand. They failed to realise that, instead of condemning the machines, they should have tried to produce designs which were suitable to mechanisation. The following contemporary quotation sums up the attitude of the Arts and Crafts Movement towards the use of machinery in furniture making:

'The introduction of machinery for moulding, which left only the fitting and polishing to be done by the craftsman, and which enabled manufacturers to produce two or three cabinets in the time formerly occupied in the making of one, was all against the quality and stability of the work. No good work was ever done in a hurry: the craftsman may be rapid, but his rapidity is the result of very deliberate thought and not of hurry. Good furniture, however, cannot be made rapidly.'

If only they had sought to understand the machine and allowed its influence to play its part in furniture design, then the furniture of the Arts and Crafts Movement would have been available for the masses, and an original contemporary style, which could have been adopted by the whole furniture trade, might have come about. The woodworking machine was a tool that was actuated by steam and not by hand; it speeded up production; it reduced the hours spent by the workman and it was more accurate in its execution. The problem was to design furniture that lent itself to machine production. What was not wanted was that the machine should be 'mastered'; the danger of this was that the production of furniture had all the appearance of handwork but was machine-made.

This was a deception practised by the Victorian furniture trade. For example, to the lay mind carving is manual work, but the carving machine did most of the work and only the final touching-up was by hand. Neither the furniture makers, who used woodworking machinery, nor the members of the Arts and Crafts, who condemned it, understood the real purport of the machine; it took future generations to realise the machine's influence on design.

In spite of their failure to produce furniture which could be bought as they had hoped by the poorer members of the community, the designers within the Arts and Crafts Movement created a new and significant style. In spite of the fact that the inspiration of their earliest members, such as Morris and Webb, was drawn from simple Gothic furniture and the simple craft of the joiner, the movement now tended to produce more elaborate furniture. One of the basic ideas of the movement was that designers and craftsmen in different branches of the decorative arts should work closely together within a group. The idea went even further than this and there was a wish to combine together the efforts of several trades in one piece.

Furniture, especially sideboards and cabinets, lent itself to this treatment. Pieces which had formerly been entirely simple and made by the joiner alone could not expect to remain the same if the tile-makers, painters and workers in leather, stained glass and metals, started to include their products in the furniture. This inclusion of the work of other artists and craftsmen in a piece of furniture was a prominent feature of the furniture made by the Arts and Crafts Movement.

A further result of this was that the movement tended to produce individual pieces such as cabinets, sideboards and tables which gave the greatest opportunity for including the work of designers in other materials and of producing fine 'art' pieces. The movement as a whole shirked the necessity for designing the essential pieces of furniture which were required by the public at this date, such as dining room and bedroom suites; they inclined to forget that furniture was for use and not only for decoration.

The Arts and Crafts Society made a point of emphasising the importance of the craftsman who made the piece of furniture and also of giving recognition as well to the designer, thereby cutting out the middleman. It was for this reason that in their Exhibition catalogues the names of both designer and craftsman were given. In the 1893 Exhibition there was an inlaid walnut cabinet which, according to the description, was designed by W. R. Lethaby and executed by A. Thorn; and, again, an inlaid sideboard was described as designed by Reginald Blomfield and executed by G. A. Mason.

The altruistic attitude of the Society was well summed up by Walter Crane, the President, in a letter to *The Cabinet Maker and Art Furnisher* in answer to the editor's criticism that the furniture was exhibited by vendors or designers rather than by the 'actual producers' or craftsmen:

'I beg to acknowledge your courtesy in sending me a copy of the journal containing an article on the Arts and Crafts Exhibition, in which I am naturally interested.

'That the Exhibition is not perfect or complete, as an exponent of the principles enunciated in my preface, I should be the first to allow; but there is a note in the catalogue especially addressed to those designers and executants whose names have been inadvertently omitted.

'I do say, however—and it is a gratifying thing it has been generally recognised by the press and the public—that ours, with all its shortcomings, is a genuine attempt to work on truer principles in the Arts and Crafts. As far as I am able, with the help of my excellent colleagues, I shall do the utmost to carry the movement forward.

'I am not unmindful of the vast trade organisation which exists between the producer and consumer, but it seems to me that arts and handicrafts have suffered under it. My idea is still the workshop where the artist or craftsman, working singly or in co-operation with his fellows, produces things of use and beauty for use rather than for profit. We may be a long way from this, but ideals, nevertheless, have their practical value as stimulants.

'The real distinction between the purely artistic spirit and the purely commercial spirit, it seems to me, lies in this: that, whereas the artist is thinking how much he can give, for love or money, the trader is thinking how little he can give, and for money alone. As the result of a little mixing we may get a compromise, but, broadly speaking, the distinction remains.'

In the Arts and Crafts Exhibition held in 1890 the members invited a number of leading London furniture makers—Gillow, Howard, Gregory, Collinson and Locke, Cooper and Liberty—to exhibit. But at the next Exhibition either they refused or were not invited, which suggests that they were unable to come to agreement with the Society over the recognition of the various craftsmen who helped to make the furniture.

In spite of their failure to understand mechanisation and to design for the requirements of the poorer public, whom they wished to help, one must respect the Arts and Crafts Society for the work that it did to improve the standard of the design of the decorative arts and the position of the craftsman and designer.

As we have said, the various conflicting trends within the Arts and Crafts Movement, and the respective influence of its many members, is a large and specialised subject; there is still much furniture that was designed by leading members of the movement which has not yet been traced, and until this is catalogued it is not possible to assess their work accurately.

Here it is possible only to consider the work of some of the more prominent members. We have already discussed the influence of Morris and his first furniture designer, Philip Webb. In about 1890 he was succeeded by his pupil, George Jack (1855–1932) as the chief designer for Morris & Co. The pieces designed by Jack had little relation to Webb's furniture or the original ideals of design of the Morris Movement. Most of Jack's furniture was plain in outline and made of walnut or mahogany of the highest quality; the pieces relied for their decoration on highly elaborate panels of floral marquetry. A typical piece is illustrated in Fig. 88. This furniture was costly and could never have gone into anything but a wealthy man's home.

In spite of the deviation of George Jack, the tradition of Philip Webb's joined furniture did not die out. Sydney Barnsley, on his retreat to the Cotswolds in 1893, continued to make furniture of this simple joined construction, which met a small but appreciative demand. Barnsley, together with Ernest Gimson, Mervyn Macartney and W. R. Lethaby, had formed Kenton & Co. in 1890. This firm was artistically successful, but came to an end in 1892 for financial reasons; after its close some of it members moved to Gloucestershire where they worked together in the same area, either in partnership or closely associated. The members of this Cotswold School, as it came to be called, followed closely in the early Morris tradition and believed that a detailed knowledge of the methods of construction and an absolute understanding of the use of materials were essential.

Another member of Kenton & Co., W. R. Lethaby (1857–1931), architect and designer, was greatly influenced by Philip Webb. The furniture he designed was simple and unpolished and clearly shows Webb's influence, but unlike Webb he used floral marquetry to decorate his simple oak pieces. Lethaby's marquetry, however, differs from that used by George Jack, as can be seen by comparing Figs. 88 and 89. Lethaby also designed more conventional furniture in mahogany and rosewood which had no connection with the accepted style of the Arts and Crafts Movement.

Ernest Gimson (1864–1919), architect and designer, was a close friend of Ernest Barnsley (Sydney's brother) and for a while in Gloucestershire they were in partnership. His furniture was perhaps the most original and least derivative of any of the members of the Arts and Crafts Movement. The outlines of his pieces were supremely simple, light and elegant. They had large, plain surfaces which were nearly always elaborately decorated. It is possible to see a certain similarity between his work and that of George Jack, for both combined simplicity of form with elaborate decoration.

The architect and designer, C. R. Ashbee (1863–1942), was another prominent member of the Arts and Crafts Movement. He was chief designer of the Guild of Handicraft and in 1904 founded the School of Arts and Crafts at Chipping Camden. So far little of Ashbee's work has been traced, but one of the pieces that has been found is illustrated in Fig. 90.

Coincident with the Arts and Crafts, a new style of ornament began to make its appearance in wallpapers, fabrics, bookbindings, metalwork and furniture. It was called *Art Nouveau*, although it owed its origin to England. It was a style consisting chiefly of naturalistic forms of trees, branches, foliage and flowers, sometimes combined with slender female figures, which were the contribution of the Pre-Raphaelites. In furniture the floral motifs of tulips on long tenuous stalks or symmetrical trees were used in applied beaten metalwork, or more often inlaid or painted. Sometimes the structure of the furniture was shaped with the long undulating curves of the style. Such sinuous lines did not lend themselves to being happily translated in wood, for it was an unsound construction owing to the short grain left by the curve.

Two distinguished architects, Charles F. Voysey (1857–1941) and Charles Rennie Mackintosh, were exponents of the style and designed wallpapers, fabrics and furniture. The former, who was also a member of the Arts and Crafts Society, gave to his furniture an original character. It was austere, straight lined and with little ornament. Voysey was very fond of the motif of the heart, which he used in applied metal as key-plates, in strap hinges, and even as a letterbox plate. In furniture the heart shape was cut out; he used it not only on the backs of chairs, but also on the simple banisters of his staircases. This cut-out heart was not an original idea for it was a popular ornament for window shutters in the 18th century. An example of his work is illustrated in Fig. 91.

On the other hand, the *Art Nouveau* furniture of Charles Rennie Mackintosh was less happy than that of Voysey; the narrow and tall backs of his chairs were too exaggerated and his fitted corner seats and chimney-pieces with their curved rails, which were considered original at the time, have today a somewhat melancholy look (see Figs. 92 and 93).

The most extravagant designs of decoration and furniture in the *Art Nouveau* style took place on the Continent in the early years of the 20th century. In England after 1900 the style had lost favour and therefore there was no further development. Evidence of the actual dislike of *Art Nouveau* is to be found in an interesting letter to *The Times* quoted by Dr Tschudi Madsen in his monumental work, *Sources of Art Nouveau* (1956). This letter of 15th April, 1901, was a protest against the Victoria and Albert Museum employing a gift of several thousand pounds, which they received in 1901 from the eminent art dealer and connoisseur, Sir George Donaldson, 'for the purchase of the best models of the style called New Art'. The letter ran:

'It is much to be regretted that the authorities of South Kensington have introduced into the Museum specimens of the work styled "l'Art Nouveau".

'This work is neither right in principle nor does it evince a proper regard for the material employed. As cabinet-maker's work it is badly executed. It represents only a trick of design which, developed from debased forms, has prejudicially affected the design of furniture and buildings in neighbouring countries.

'In its present position it is in danger of being looked upon as a recognised model which has received the approval of the authorities for study by students and designers, and the harm it may thus produce on our national art cannot be easily gauged.

'We, the undersigned, desire publicly to protest against its importation at South Kensington, and most strongly against its recommendation by the authorities to the notice of furniture makers and others.'

The signatures were: John Belcher, A.R.A., Reginald Blomfield, Mervyn Macartney and Edward S. Prior.

Besides the pieces which such men as C. R. Ashbee, Baillie Scott and C. F. Voysey designed for their clients, furniture dating from the 17th and 18th centuries again became popular and was considered suitable to mix with the productions of the Arts and Crafts Movement. The dealers in old furniture were prospering, for the collecting of antiques was becoming fashionable

—particularly with the man whose wealth was comparatively newly acquired and who wanted to furnish his country mansion.

With architect members of the Arts and Crafts Movement, the inglenook, with its seats flanking the fire, was much in evidence. Furniture and decoration were often a combination of design inspired by the 17th century, together with painted friezes, wallpapers and curtains decorated with *Art Nouveau* patterns. These country houses were a picturesque medley of gable roofs, tall and massive chimney-stacks, and casement windows with leaded lights. If the house was not of the 17th-century style, then it was that of Queen Anne with red brick, hipped gables and sash windows divided into small rectangular panes. Norman Shaw was the chief exponent of the Queen Anne style in the last decade of the 19th century. The houses built for the wealthy were lavishly fitted with expensive staircases, panelling and chimney-pieces.

Whatever the architects designed in the way of furniture was soon copied by the furniture trade, first of all by the West End firms and then by the cheaper shops or furnishing stores supplied by the East End manufacturers. In this process the restrained and pleasing design of the architect developed into furniture that was over-accentuated in form and vulgarised by lavish ornament either carved or inlaid. The trade paper, *The Cabinet Maker and Furnisher*, during the period it was criticising the Arts and Crafts Exhibition, illustrated each month several pages of 'original designs' by a hack designer called Henry Pringuer. It is strange that the editor of this paper should have possessed so little sensitivity towards furniture design that he allowed this designer's furniture, overloaded with ornament, to appear.

In one of the issues a letter is published from a firm of cabinet-makers and upholsterers protesting about Pringuer's furniture, saying that some of his designs are 'simply outrageous', and that as there has been a surfeit of designs by this artist in *The Cabinet Maker*, surely a change is now desirable. Pringuer, in his published reply to this complaint, sums up his furniture by saying: 'I range from solid English Jacobean to fanciful French.' *The Furniture Gazette* was also publishing equally bad furniture designs by A. Jonquet as an inspiration to manufacturers.

A new style came into being called the 'Quaint Style'. This was a pot-pourri of the Japanese style, the Arts and Crafts and *Art Nouveau*, the latter taken from its worst Continental extravagances. It was not adopted, however, by all the furniture trade, for such shops as Heal & Son and the Bath Cabinet Makers produced furniture of a plain and simple design showing that they had not been unmindful of the teachings of the Arts and Crafts Society concerning design.

A study of the furniture of Heal & Son, mostly the work of its chief designer, the late Sir Ambrose Heal, belongs more properly to the 20th century; however, certain pieces were made in the Victorian era and two such are illustrated in Figs. 94 and 95.

Apart from a few firms and the work produced by the Arts and Crafts Movement, the furniture trade in this last decade of the Victorian era produced goods about which the only remarkable thing was the poverty of design. In the early and middle Victorian periods, in spite of the weakness of much of the commercial furniture design, there were compensating features. For instance, firms like Jackson and Graham and Wright and Mansfield were producing 'masterpieces' in the form of sideboards or cabinets. It is true that these pieces were mainly for exhibition and they could not therefore be considered typical. However, professionals were engaged to produce the design, and the most skilled craftsmen were employed in order that the quality of the carving, inlaying and cabinet work might be of the highest order.

These exhibition pieces and other furniture of the first quality were a revelation and inspiration to the public and the general furniture trade. In the last decade of the Queen's reign, outside the Arts and Crafts Movement, this desire to produce outstanding pieces of furniture no longer existed.

CHAPTER FOUR

The Victorian Home

THERE was not a great deal of difference between the homes of the richer classes in the Victorian period and similar houses in the 18th century. Families were large and accordingly the houses had to be designed to accommodate them. This meant that there were many bedrooms and dressing rooms besides the usual reception rooms. The reception rooms would include a drawing room, morning room, dining room and possibly a library and study; in the great houses there were, of course, even more reception rooms. In the large Victorian houses there were, however, two quite noticeable features which made them distinguishable from their counterparts built in the 18th century.

The first difference was the increase in size of the servants' quarters. The vastly increased wealth, brought about by the Industrial Revolution and the easier means of transport, encouraged people to entertain large house parties. These would often continue for long periods and as some guests left others would arrive. To run a house with many visitors and with the high standard of comfort which the Victorian expected needed a greatly increased number of staff. It would also be quite usual for a visiting gentleman to bring his valet and a visiting lady her maid. If children were also invited, they would come with their nurse and possibly a nursery maid or governess.

In Victorian times servants attained a standard of efficiency that will probably never be surpassed. An elaborate etiquette grew up in the servants' hall and the duties performed by each member of the household became clearly established; a butler in a large house in Cornwall would fulfil nearly identical duties as a butler in a large house in Scotland. In the servants' hall at meals each member of the household would sit in strict order of precedence, and the visiting servants would take the precedence of their employers. At meals the lower servants would take their places first and the upper servants, who changed for dinner, would enter in pairs. After the meat course had been eaten, the upper servants would rise and their pudding would be served to them in the housekeeper's room. These privileges, which were jealously guarded, could still be found in some great English country houses until 1939. All this necessitated a considerable increase in the servants' quarters, which in the larger houses would include a kitchen, scullery, butler's pantry, larder, stillroom, lamproom, brushing room, housekeeper's room, steward's room, servants' hall and innumerable servants' bedrooms.

The second difference between the wealthy Victorian home and that of the 18th century was the inclusion of a few new rooms with a specific purpose. During the 19th century the game of billiards became a fashionable recreation and a billiard room became an almost essential feature of the Victorian country house. Men in the upper classes had also taken to smoking, hence the smoking room or tower became another necessary apartment. Towards the end of the Victorian era the strict necessity for using this room became less, and smoking in other parts of the house became accepted. It was a considerable time, however, before smoking in the drawing room was allowed, and it was even then essential to ask permission of the hostess. It was not considered proper for women to enter the smoking room, and this, rather more than the unacceptability of smoking, was probably the reason for their popularity after there was no longer a strict social necessity for using them.

Because of the Victorian love of flowers and plant life, the conservatory attached to the house (usually leading off one of the ground floor rooms such as a drawing or morning room) became popular with both the upper and middle classes. In some country mansions, on account of its large dimensions and imposing appearance, it was termed a 'winter garden'. In London in the smaller house, space did not permit a conservatory, but this was overcome by building glass boxes or 'miniature greenhouses', particularly on landings, in the place of the normal window. Such a structure is illustrated in Fig. 96.

A very good example of a house which was converted into a mansion by the building of two new wings is Somerley, the Hampshire home of the Earl of Normanton. In 1850 a spacious drawing room and a large picture gallery, nearly 100 feet long and 50 feet wide, were built. They formed a new wing on one side of the old house, which had been built in the last decade of the 18th century from the designs of Samuel Wyatt. The third Earl, feeling that the house was still not large enough and lacked rooms essential to the social life of his time, added in 1868–1870 another wing, planned with a large smoking room, an open court, a conservatory, and a billiard room.

Stradey Castle, Llanelly, South Wales (Fig. 97), is an entirely Victorian mansion. The main block of the house was built in 1840 and the Tower block, which can be seen in the background, was added in 1874. This house contains all the typical Victorian reception rooms, including a large hall in the Elizabethan style and very extensive servants' quarters. Two of the main rooms, the dining room and the drawing room, are illustrated in Figs. 108 and 109. These interior photographs are reproduced from plates taken in the late 19th century by C. R. Mansel Lewis, the present owner's father, and so they provide exact contemporary evidence of how the rooms were furnished.

The houses of the middle classes also had large rooms, but they were naturally planned for less entertaining and for fewer servants. In the wealthy home a multiplicity of rooms existed, each for a different purpose, whereas in the middle-class home the rooms were often made to serve two purposes.

In a town house, the larger it was, the greater were the number of the stories and the more arduous the work of the servants. In the 18th century the wealthy man who was incapacitated by ill-health was carried upstairs in a chair by two footmen. In the Victorian period, however, the domestic lift, as we know from advertisements, was in use at least in the 1850s. Even if the house had a lift, it would mainly be for the owner and his family; most of the food and hot water would be carried up and down many flights of stairs by the servants.

In both the 18th and 19th centuries the heating of the rooms was the same—coal fires—but in the sphere of lighting there was a considerable change during the Victorian period. Candles were no longer the principal means of lighting, for during the century there was an evolution from candles to colza oil lamps, and from colza oil to paraffin, and from paraffin to gas, and finally to electricity. In country mansions private gas installations were fitted, and later the same happened with electricity. It is still today possible to find country houses which make their own electricity.

Sanitation also showed many signs of improvement. During the last half of Victoria's reign, even in a fairly small house, the bathroom was an integral feature of the plan. The old-fashioned portable bath, the hot water for which was carried up from the basement, or the bath with the water heated by a 'bath stove' (the flue of which went up the chimney of the bedroom or dressing room) was superseded by a fixed bath with hot and cold water supplied from a main source.

In the 18th century in the houses of the upper classes water closets had not been unusual, but they were not satisfactory because the sealed trap had not been invented. With the use of this trap, which prevented smell coming from the drain, water closets—even in small middle-class homes—were considered a necessity, certainly where there was main drainage or a cesspool. In many country districts, owing to the lack of public sanitation, no such thing as a water closet existed; and this, of course, is still true today in some English villages, where the inhabitants have to rely on a chemical or earth closet.

The stables were an essential part of both the 18th-century and the Victorian home, and the country mansion had its stable yard with its riding and coach horses, carriages, coachmen and grooms. The same also applied to the town mansion, where the stables were situated in a mews at the back of the house. In London this only applied to the houses of the wealthy; the majority of the middle class were not in a position to keep a carriage. The term 'carriage trade' is still sometimes used by shopkeepers to describe a high-class clientele; for to keep a carriage, especially in London, was a costly affair and could be afforded only by the richest people.

Servants were the foundation upon which the whole social structure of the Victorian home was erected. Without them there could have been no dining rooms distant from the kitchen, no cluttered drawing rooms that required lengthy daily dusting, no coal fires in every bedroom, and no London streets with mile after mile of three- and four-storied houses, each with its basement and its 'below stairs' world.

Between twenty and thirty servants were considered essential for the running of a really large house. The late 19th-century photograph (Fig. 98) of the Duke of Westminster's indoor household at Eaton Hall shows an unusually large staff of forty. There are seventeen women, including the housekeeper and the Duchess's personal maid. Neither the steward, the under butler, the clerk of the works, nor the Duke's private secretary, who were employed at this date, are in the photograph; probably because they were considered too important to be included in a group with the general staff. There are several footmen, a hall porter, two grooms of the chambers, a chef and two under-chefs.

Seven of the men formed a private Fire Brigade and they can be seen in their very handsome uniforms. Besides their obvious duties in the case of fire, these men had many other jobs; they would fill and carry the coal buckets and wood baskets, an enormous task in a house of this size before central heating; they would carry the luggage of arriving and departing guests; they would be responsible for the removal of all household rubbish; one of them would be on duty as a night watchman to guard against fire, to answer bells or open the front door to late arrivals.

Towards the end of the 19th century it was no longer usual for footmen to powder their hair or to wear knee breeches when they were in the country. However, when they moved with the family to London, this practice still continued.

Even in the homes of the lower middle class there were usually one or two female servants. A firm of furniture makers, Messrs Leverton, in an advertisement of 1855, estimated the cost of furnishing a six-roomed house at £67 17s. 7d., of which £4 18s. od. was scheduled for the outlay on the servant's bedroom. In a slightly larger house, where the furnishing estimate was £138 12s. 5d., there was an allowance made for the furnishing of two servants' bedrooms. A catalogue some years later of Holland & Sons, of 23, Mount Street, London, lists a Servant's Set, which ranged in price from £4 19s. 2d. to £8 12s. 2d. according to quality. This set comprised an iron bedstead and a set of bedding, a japanned oak-colour chest of drawers, a toilet glass, a japanned oak-colour washstand and set of toilet ware, a cane-seated chair, a towel rail and a clothes rack. Although there is no suggestion of luxury in this, it can be seen that fairly adequate provision was made for the necessities.

Out of a three-volume book by H. C. Davidson, *The Home* (1900), nearly one whole volume is devoted to the treatment of servants; the laws of master and servant, the engagement of servants, their various duties, and their rights, perquisites, allowances and leisure. Cassell's *Household Guide* (1880) gives one an idea of the duties which were expected from a housemaid employed in the ordinary Victorian home:

'A good housemaid will rise at six, and have her grates cleaned and rooms swept by seven. She will then go upstairs, wash her hands and make herself tidy for taking to the bedroom hot water if required to do so. In the meanwhile, the dust will have settled, and the rooms will be ready on her return to be finished by eight. By nine o'clock breakfast ought to be cleared away and the housemaid ready to strip the beds, empty the slops, and set the bedrooms in order. By eleven o'clock the upstairs work ought to be done, unless extra cleaning is in question. Washing up china and glass, dusting the drawing room, and other light labour of the kind may take till twelve or one o'clock, by which time a housemaid ought to be dressed for the day, fit to answer the door, wait on the family and do needle-work. Any work required of the servant after mid-day should be of a nature not to soil her garments.

'At dusk, it is a housemaid's place to close all the windows at the upper part of the house. Before going to bed she has to turn down all the beds of the family, replenish ewers and water bottles, empty slops, and put everything in its place. If she has the charge of the plate-basket she carries it to the master's room, together with hot water. Considerate employers will dispense with a housemaid's attendance by ten o'clock, bearing in mind her morning duties.'

For these considerable duties *The Household Guide* goes on to say ' . . . in most country places £10 to £14 per annum is the usual amount to pay'.

Fitted wash-basins, modern bathrooms, improved methods of cleaning and heating—all these would have been earlier on the scene had there been any real necessity for them. So long as there were plenty of men and women available to fetch and carry, the development of labour-saving devices was unnecessary. The elaborateness and the ornateness of the Victorian home was made possible only by the ready supply of domestic servants.

The difference between our life and that of our Victorian ancestors is so great that there is hardly anything common to the homes of both periods, except that we still have beds, tables and chairs. Also little remains of the elaborate and formal entertaining—the 'at homes', the long dinners, private balls, garden parties and musical evenings.

A consideration of the Victorian home room by room will help to give a clearer picture, both of the way of life that went on and of the more or less standard furniture which could be found in each part of the house.

Space demands that discussion must be confined to the use of the rooms and the furniture that was to be found in them. It must be realised, however, that furniture was no longer almost alone in these rooms. Pictures, silver and porcelain in the 18th and early 19th centuries helped to create the general effect in a room, but in the Victorian period the volume of these decorative objects greatly increased, and the room now also contained bronzes, miniatures, souvenirs, trophies, together with a profusion of vases, jars, lamps and knick-knacks.

There were photographs in silver frames, little boxes and carefully placed piles of books, stained glass windows, potted palms and vases of flowers; there were animals in cases and innumerable objects often made in wax or paper placed under glass domes. A consideration of all these could not be included within the scope of this book.

The drawing rooms at 18, Stafford Terrace and Stradey Castle (frontispiece and Fig. 109) give an idea of the general setting of such rooms in the 1870s. It can be seen at once that although there is plenty of conventional furniture it no longer stands alone and uncluttered as it had done in previous centuries; it is against this background that most Victorian furniture must be considered.

Even when the Victorians took as their inspiration the crisp, clean style of Adam, the result was something very different from the neo-classic style of the 1770s. The Victorian version of a drawing room in this manner is illustrated in Fig. 84.

The Victorian entrance hall presented so many variations in its size, decoration and furniture that it could almost be taken as a distinguishing feature of the social class to which the owner of the house belonged. It ranged from a narrow passage-like area, with the staircase and the ground floor rooms leading off, to the spacious and imposing apartment of the wealthy man's mansion, when it often took on the character of a large and lofty hall, two stories in height, with the staircase apart or with a double staircase descending to the centre of the room.

In the narrow hall of the ordinary Victorian home there were several pieces of essential furniture, perhaps the most important of which was the stand for coats, hats and umbrellas. This piece of furniture was not mentioned by Sheraton in his *Cabinet Dictionary*, and the earliest representation of it appears to be a colour plate in *Ackerman's Repository of the Arts*, published in 1812, where it is termed a 'cloak stand'. It was designed in the form of a free-standing pillar from which protruded at the top turned pegs for hanging hats and coats. Half way up the column was fixed a circular support pierced to hold upright umbrellas and sticks. At the base was a tin tray to collect the water from wet umbrellas.

An alternative design was the stand that stood against the wall. It had flat wood arms branching from a centre upright, upon which were screwed coat and hat hooks. An example taken from one of William Smee's early catalogues is shown in Fig. 99. Later, some ingenious designer thought of combining the hat-stand with a table in the middle, on which was placed the card tray. Below the table top there was a drawer for the clothes and hat brushes; there was a mirror attached to the table top, so that people could see what they looked like before going out, or guests could tidy themselves before entering the drawing room.

Sometimes, instead of the table, a bench formed part of the structure, on each side of which were stands for umbrellas and sticks (Fig. 100). The large number of surviving hat and coat stands of many different designs and woods (chiefly among which were rosewood, mahogany and oak) shows how essential this piece of furniture was considered by the Victorian middle class.

Another important piece of hall furniture, if it was not incorporated in the hat-stand, was a narrow table which stood against the wall. Upon it was placed a bowl or salver for visitors' cards. The strict etiquette of the Victorian world is brought home to us by the mention of the custom of 'calling' and leaving a card. If their friends were not at home, the visitors handed the servant their visiting-cards. Cassell's *Household Guide* (*circa* 1880) contains the etiquette on the subject:

> 'A lady should always be prepared to receive visitors, if at home, between the hours of three and five o'clock . . . When making a ceremonious morning call a gentleman should take his hat with him into the drawing room, and when there should hold it in his hand in an easy manner. It is not now necessary for a gentleman to take off his gloves, if they are particularly well-fitting and of light colour.'

There were many more ramifications to the procedure for leaving cards. Cards were left on a hostess after she had given a ball or a dinner. If the caller were a married lady, she would leave her own card, and her husband's card if the lady on whom she was calling was also married. The custom, of course, continued long after the Victorian era.

The hall chair goes back to the first half of the 18th century. Sheraton says that they were 'placed in halls, for the use of servants or strangers waiting on business'. The chair of Sheraton's time and earlier invariably had a wooden seat and back, the crest of the family being painted in a panel upon the latter.

The fashion of the hall chair being painted with the family crest on the back was continued late into the 19th century. It seems natural that the nobleman of the 18th century should adorn the backs of his hall chairs with his crest or coat of arms; it has more than a trace of snobbism, however, when the custom was copied by the Victorian bourgeois in whose case one cannot but suspect that he was eager to claim an ancestry setting him apart as being better bred than his neighbours.

The hall table, chairs and benches in the first half of the Victorian period were either in the Grecian or the Elizabethan style, mahogany being used for the former and oak, usually polished a bright yellow, for the latter. An oak bench and table which are part of a hall suite for a large house are illustrated in Figs. 102 and 103. Stained black oak furniture in the 'Elizabethan style', coarsely carved, was also often used in the Victorian hall, and hall chairs with Gothic backs were not uncommon.

The 18th-century custom of having a long-case clock in the hall continued throughout the Victorian era, either in a mahogany or oak case, with a 7-day or 30-hour movement. A long-case clock with Westminster chimes became popular in the late Victorian period. Companion to the clock was that essential instrument for forecasting the English weather, the barometer. The familiar banjo barometer continued to be used in Victorian times even after the far more reliable aneroid barometer became popular. The aneroid barometer had been in use in France as early as 1750, but it was not until the 1860s that it came into general use in London.

In the more wealthy home the dining room was reserved for luncheon and dinner, and also for breakfast, unless there was a breakfast room as well. In the middle-class home, however, the dining room was not a stately and imposing apartment for large dinner parties, but a more family room. It was used not only for meals, but also as a sitting room, perhaps more particularly by the master of the house, who would use it for reading and writing letters. The following extract from Holland & Sons' catalogue, published in the last quarter of the 19th century, gives an exact idea of the dual purpose of the dining room. There is also a drawing of the room illustrated in Fig. 104.

> 'This room is so arranged as to be suitable either as dining or sitting room, and can be furnished completely for £100. The articles included are enumerated below: A sideboard book-case, a dining table, 6 dining chairs, a writing table, 2 easy chairs, a corner cabinet, a pair of tapestry curtains, a Brussels carpet.'

The fact that the catalogue advertises the room as completely furnished for £100 confirms the fact that this arrangement was only used in the smaller home. The same catalogue contains both an illustration and prices for a larger, more formal dining room which was more expensive, but did not include easy chairs, writing tables or book cases as suitable furniture.

The most important piece of furniture in the dining room was the sideboard. This is corroborated by a writer in an article in the *Art Journal Illustrated Catalogue* of the Paris Exhibition of 1867:

> 'The dining room furniture of England, as distinguished from the furniture suited to a drawing room, should be substantial, massive, handsome, and in colour somewhat sombre rather than gay. The sideboard is the *pièce de résistance*, in which these characteristics usually reach a climax; this is the article in which dinner-giving Englishmen take a pride, and, as usual, our cabinet-makers here put out their utmost strength.'

This importance of the sideboard is exemplified in the Great Exhibition and in the other International Exhibitions, where many examples were exhibited by all the best firms of English cabinet-makers. The examples made by the Warwickshire and other carvers (Figs. 16–22) show to what degree of extravagance this piece of furniture could obtain.

From mediaeval times the sideboard was always 'the board' upon which were placed the vessels and cups for drinking. It was also used as a place for the display of the gilt and silver plate of the household. This use continued up to the time of Sheraton, for the late 18th-century sideboard was fitted with a brass rail against which the dishes and salvers could stand in an upright position (Fig. 2). During the Victorian era the use of the sideboard to display the dining room plate declined; this piece of furniture now became more ornate and in mid-Victorian times the sideboard had a carved back in which a mirror was fitted.

Drawings of elaborate exhibition pieces in this style are shown in Figs 48 and 49. A somewhat later and more modest example can be seen in the background of Fig. 105. A plainer, but high quality example of a sideboard with a mirror back is illustrated in Fig. 106. As a very general rule it can be said that the earliest Victorian sideboards were of the pedestal type, in which the top, fitted with drawers, spanned twin pedestals; in the space in the middle there was room to stand the cellaret. In the 1860s this space was enclosed by doors to form a cupboard (Fig. 106). Later the pedestal effect in many cases disappeared altogether.

Throughout the Victorian period the sideboard followed the old tradition of being the drink board or table upon which were placed the decanters and wine bottles. It was not used for carving the joint, for in the Victorian middle-class home this was done from the dining table by the master of the house, who sat at one end and his wife at the other. It is for this reason that the armchairs in which they sat were known as 'carvers'. Other members of the family, and guests, sat in single chairs.

The Victorian dining table was upheld on four stout turned legs. It was capable of being extended by the addition of extra leaves to allow for more places to be set (Figs. 101, 105 and 108). These tables could have square (Figs. 105 and 108) or rounded (Fig. 104) ends. In 'period' tables in Jacobean and Elizabethan styles, besides the frieze and legs, the table edge might be carved also (Fig. 105). A table of this type was known as a 'telescopic table' and Eastlake in his *Household Taste* had some satirical comments to make on its design:

> 'It is generally made of planks of polished oak or mahogany, laid upon an insecure framework of the same material, and supported by four gouty legs, ornamented by the turner with mouldings, which look like inverted cups and saucers piled upon an attic baluster. . . . Such a table cannot be soundly made in the sense that ordinary furniture is sound. When it is extended it looks weak and untidy at the sides; when it is reduced to its shortest length the legs appear heavy and ill-proportioned. It is always liable to get out of order, and from the very nature of its construction must be an inartistic object.'

What, however, Eastlake forgot was that the Victorian dining table was comfortable to sit at, for there were no legs in the way, except at the extreme corners where no one sat. Dining tables were covered by a table cloth when in use and by a cover at other times made perhaps of velvet, baize or linen. It was no longer the custom, as it had been in the 18th century, to remove the cloth for dessert. This is confirmed by Cassell's *Household Guide*: 'The table cloth is now almost invariably left on the table for dessert. This plan saves a great deal of trouble and on that account is to be recommended.'

Although the majority of Victorian dining tables were rectangular and made on the extending basis, circular tables were not unknown. Such a table is illustrated in Figs. 110 and 111. The latter figure shows the table ready to take the additional slips of wood which will increase its circumference and thus enable more people to sit at it.

Dining room chairs, however, were by no means so standard in pattern, and a number of different styles were current at various times throughout the Victorian era. A dining chair of the earliest Victorian type is shown in Fig. 116, but the chair with a balloon back and turned front legs (Figs. 112–115) quickly became more popular. The feature of this chair was the great comfort of the back. The oval supported not only the shoulders but also the middle of one's back exactly where required. The back rails of the chair were curved to make it even more comfortable.

There is no question that out of all the English chairs with wooden backs from earliest to modern times, the balloon chair was one of the most comfortable. It continued to be popular for a considerable time, for it is much illustrated in trade catalogues of the late 1860s; it was still being made in the 1890s, although at this time it was no longer fashionable. It was superseded first by the dining chair with an upholstered back (Figs. 117, 118 and 119 and background of Fig. 123) and then by chairs inspired by Chippendale, Hepplewhite and Sheraton designs (Fig. 83).

Dining chairs were often unrelated to the general trend, especially in large houses where the style of the chair was suited to the owner's taste or the decoration of the room. The dining room at Stradey Castle (Fig. 108) has a large set of so-called 'Elizabethan style' chairs and there is a somewhat plainer set at Charlecote Park, Warwickshire (Fig. 17).

Other pieces of dining room furniture were side tables or buffets and dinner wagons on wheels. The side table usually had two or three tiers (Fig. 122). They were used by the servants to place the dishes and plates on at the end of one course prior to serving another. The dinner wagon was for taking the food and plates to the dining room and afterwards returning them to the kitchen.

In the Victorian period a great many of the dishes were still placed on the dining table as in the 18th century. The butler's tray was essential in the larger Victorian home. It was a tray which generally had drop sides and a separate stand; a drawing from a trade catalogue of about 1850 is illustrated in Fig. 120. It could be used either in the dining room for the removal of glass and silver or as a movable table for light refreshment or as an extra table for drawing room tea. The rather less usual type of butler's tray (Fig. 121) was certainly for use at tea and in the main rooms and was not intended to be used by the servants about their duties.

The main lighting of the dining room was by a chandelier hung in the centre of the ceiling. The Victorians did not sit so long over their wine after the ladies had retired. This habit, together with the improvement of the water closet, meant that a chamber pot was no longer kept handy in a cupboard in the sideboard as had been the custom up to the beginning of Victoria's reign.

Towards the end of the century cheap oak furniture for dining rooms was particularly in evidence, coarsely carved and stained black. This was the last phase of the Elizabethan style. At the same time 'Art Furniture' was much in fashion and a page of designs published in 1877 for a dining room by E. W. Godwin is shown in Fig. 124.

The morning room, as we have seen, belonged more to the wealthy than to the middle-class home. It was a more homely sitting room, where the family could sit together or follow their pursuits such as sewing, drawing, playing cards or compiling a scrap book. In such a house the drawing room would be kept for entertaining guests or for the family sitting together immediately before or after dinner. The chiffonier (Figs. 125 and 126) and the circular-topped loo table belonged to the early and mid-Victorian morning room. Card tables were also a part of the furniture. A pair of card tables, a circular centre table, a pedestal jardinière and a set of chairs made *en suite*, are illustrated in Figs. 127–131.

Besides a set of chairs, the morning room usually had a couch and several easy chairs. Much of the furniture in the main rooms was interchangeable and its position was a matter of personal preference by the householder; the very fine loo table illustrated in Figs. 132 and 133 would have been suitable in any reception room.

The Davenport, judging by the number illustrated in furniture catalogues and remaining today, was a very popular piece of furniture. Two examples are illustrated in Figs. 134, 135 and 136. In furnishing catalogues, if the goods were grouped in sections suitable to particular rooms, the Davenport would usually come under the heading of the drawing room. It must, however, have been useful in other downstairs rooms and also in the bedrooms of the younger members of the family. It is a piece of furniture ideally suited for a lady to write the notes and invitations which were so much a part of Victorian life. Drawers with hidden spring locks and concealed sections that sprang up when the release devise was pressed (Fig. 135) were very usual in this piece of furniture. A special drawer for pens and ink and a slide flap on which no doubt the finished letters were placed (Fig. 136) were two other fairly common features.

The walnut writing cabinet (Fig. 140) is another piece which would have been used in the drawing room, library or morning room. The front falls forward to provide the writing surface and the inside is fitted up with small drawers and pigeon holes. It is interesting to compare this cabinet, which is in the collection of Miss E. M. Thornton and made by Holland & Sons, with a nearly identical piece, also stamped Holland & Sons, illustrated in Fig. 141. As can be seen from the photograph, Miss Thornton's cabinet has fine metal inlays and an elaborate escutcheon and key, whereas the other has plain locks and is edged with contrasting wood—this makes it an altogether simpler piece. The leading furniture makers would often advertise a piece in several alternative finishes or woods; thus a piece with the same design could be sold at several different prices to meet the exact requirements of a public who were very conscious of cost.

In 1868 Mr R. N. Thornton ordered almost the entire furniture for his house—Knowle Cottage, Sidmouth, Devon—from Holland & Sons of Mount Street, London. The present owner of the furniture, Miss E. M. Thornton, is his grand-daughter. It is fortunate that the makers are still in business at Mount Street and many entries for Mr Thornton's order can be seen in the firm's books. The furniture for the whole house was of the very highest quality and many pieces are illustrated here. Much of the furniture which contained drawers is stamped with the maker's name and an example of this can be seen in Fig. 144.

Two views of the morning room at 18, Stafford Terrace are illustrated in Figs. 142 and 143. The satinwood inlaid china cabinets and the firescreens, which are on either side of the fireplace, would possibly have been intended for a drawing room. In the 1870s furniture in the style of Chippendale and Hepplewhite returned to vogue; sometimes original 18th-century pieces were used and sometimes careful copies were made by the Victorian craftsmen. This is doubtless the reason why the Stafford Terrace morning room has a suite of furniture in the Hepplewhite style and the two Adam-style china cabinets, for at the time it was furnished (1874), the inclusion of furniture in the style of the late 18th century would have been considered fashionable.

The drawing room has been defined as 'the ladies' apartment essentially'. In a house without a morning room, it was the only proper sitting room of the family and it was the room where the mistress of the house received her visitors. In smaller houses it played a very important part in the life of the family, for it was the only room suitable for entertainment, and entertainment at home was more important in Victorian days than it is today when so many attractions exist outside. At a dinner party the guests assembled there before dinner, and afterwards the ladies retired to the drawing room where they were later joined by the gentlemen. At an evening party it was the room where the guests would be entertained by singing and music. One of its essentials, therefore, was a piano and a music cabinet.

As it was a woman's rather than a man's room, the furnishing and decoration had a sense of luxury and elegance rather than comfort and solidity. The ornaments and *bric-à-brac*, the pictures and porcelains were most often to be found in the drawing room. As has been explained, this tended to minimise the importance of individual pieces of furniture. Much of the furniture of the Victorian drawing room was the work of the upholsterer, the ottoman and the pouffe being particularly in evidence. This upholstered furniture is discussed and illustrated in the chapter on Techniques and Materials (No. 5).

Perhaps the greatest impression on entering a Victorian drawing room would be of tables which were there in great numbers. They were, of course, very necessary, if surface space was to be found for displaying the multitude of objects that Victorians considered appropriate. Some of these tables can be seen in the illustrations of the interiors of drawing rooms and others are shown in Figs. 145–178.

Chairs would be the most numerous in the drawing room and besides many single chairs there would also be a set which would be somewhat similar to those in the dining room, but lighter and more elaborately decorated. This set of chairs would be used when there was a larger company to seat than could be accommodated on the sofas and upholstered chairs; they were also used for sitting at card and loo tables and for seating guests at a musical evening or similar entertainment. Some examples of chairs for the drawing room and other reception rooms are illustrated in Figs. 179–194.

Space does not permit writing in detail about each piece of drawing room furniture, but some examples are shown in Figs. 195–206 and a brief description is given in the captions.

In the larger house the drawing room, like the dining room, was of imposing and stately proportions; sometimes in London houses there was a smaller inner drawing room as well. In a country house the drawing room was on the ground floor, but in a town house in a terrace it was nearly always on the first floor. There were often large folding doors between the room at the front and the one at the back, so that both rooms could be thrown into one for an evening's entertainment. Mr Pooter in George Grossmith's *Diary of a Nobody* describes his drawing room prepared for a party: 'The arrangement of the drawing room was excellent. Carrie had hung muslin curtains over the folding doors . . .'

The Victorian house, whether it was in a terrace or standing alone, was seldom designed without its bay windows, which allowed a room (generally the drawing room) more than one aspect. Aspidistras and palms were particularly evident; a favourite position for these in the smaller house was in the bay window, where they stood in large china or brass bowls placed on a wooden stand or table. The painting of a room of about 1840 (Fig. 207) shows, in the background, a bay window and in the middle ground an opening where there may well be double doors folded back out of sight. The set of chairs, of which one is in the foreground draped with a piece of material, are typical of this date and the precursor of the fully balloon-back chair which was to become so popular by 1850.

The cosy corner was another feature of the late Victorian room, particularly the drawing room or smoking room. The cosy corner illustrated in Fig. 208 is the work of a decorating firm; a somewhat different example at Dunglass Castle (Fig. 93) is the work of the architect.

E. Knight in a pamphlet, 'Taste and Economy in Decoration and Furniture', published in 1893, is critical of these constructions and writes:

'Why we should build little summer-houses in our drawing rooms, and call them "cosy corners" or "inglenooks", passes the understanding. Where any odd corner already exists in a room, caused by some structural peculiarity of building, by all means make it as cosy as possible; but the number of flimsy wooden structures one meets with nowadays, which have no real meaning for their existence, is truly appalling. People must become tired of these dodgy nooks after a little while. The novelty is at first, no doubt, attractive, more or less, according to the beholder's constitution, and it may be greatly admired by many if seen only occasionally and for short periods. In twenty years we shall wonder how we could have admired them at all. Perhaps the concession of a corner seat with provision for books, etc. on the upper part, something like the sketch [Fig. 208], may be made to the prevailing fancy . . .'

Either drawings or photographs of some drawing rooms in different styles are illustrated in the frontispiece and Figs. 84, 109, 207, 209, 210, and 211. The details of these rooms are discussed more fully in the captions to the illustrations.

In the same way that the drawing room was essentially a woman's room, so the library was a man's. In the Victorian country house, in the absence of a business room or study, it was not only a repository for books and a place for reading and writing, but also the room in which the master of the house conducted his family affairs.

The more literary tastes the family had, so inevitably the greater the range of bookshelves, but for the average country home two or three book cases were usually sufficient. Such book cases were free-standing pieces of furniture, and were not fitted to the walls (Figs. 41, 212 and 215). The library with fitted shelves around the room was more common to the 18th than the 19th century. The library (or 'Living Room') at Sheringham Hall, Norfolk, is an example of a transitional style. Here the rosewood book cases are neither entirely free-standing nor completely fitted as part of the wall in the way they would have been in the late 18th century. These book cases, made in 1839, are illustrated in Fig. 216.

A new design of book case came into fashion in the first half of the 19th century. It was long and low, being four to five feet in height, and the top was used as a shelf for ornaments, the books being ranged on open shelves below. Sometimes these book cases were fitted with brass grilles with a silk lining behind them (Fig. 213).

After the book cases, the principal piece of furniture was a large pedestal writing table which generally stood in the bay window, or the centre of a large room. An example is illustrated in Fig. 219. Around the fireside there would be easy chairs and a couch, and the room would also contain side and centre tables to complete the furnishing. Such a library would hardly be expected in the town house of a middle-class family, in which one wing or dwarf book case in the parlour would suffice to house the family books (Fig. 217). Favourite styles for the decoration and furniture of the library were the Elizabethan, the Early English and the Gothic.

The library was not the only room to have a desk, for as explained already, in the smaller house with only two reception rooms the desk would probably be in the dining room. In the house that had a morning room but no library, the desk would probably be there. In the year 1868 the accounts show that Holland & Sons supplied two desks to Mr R. N. Thornton at Sidmouth; the kidney-shaped writing table (Fig. 221) was intended for the library and the elegant small desk (Figs. 222 and 223) for the boudoir. A somewhat similar but much lighter kidney-shaped writing table is illustrated in Fig. 224. This piece would more probably have been intended for the morning room or the drawing room. Another desk is shown in Fig. 225.

The four-post bedstead with its curtains and tester top had been considered from mediaeval times to be the most outstanding piece of furniture in the home. The appearance of the bed was much enhanced by its draperies. In mediaeval times the curtains hung from a draped tester which was suspended from the ceiling. In the 16th century the tester was held up by four posts standing on the floor. Our ancestors considered that the night air was poisonous because it was believed that it was the carrier of infection. The windows of the bedroom, therefore, had to be kept closed. It must be remembered that the plague or pestilence was a recurring disease and that its effect on mediaeval communities was so devastating that it was rightly regarded as the main hazard to life.

Therefore, it would seem that the curtains enclosing the bed were designed as a further protection. By the 19th century, however, the night air was no longer held to be a danger, although the custom of curtaining the bed still often remained. In 1826 George Smith, author of *The Cabinet-Maker and Upholsterer's Guide*, offered this explanation for the use of bed curtains:

'In a climate so variable as that of Britain, where the transitions are so sudden from cold to heat, and from wet to dry, etc., one uniform system, both as regards dress as well as the fitting up of our apartments, has been found the most beneficial and conducive to health; and in point of comfort the old English four-post bedstead, with its curtains and drapery, will always be found to claim a preference before any other, although it does not follow that it is necessary to close the curtains so effectually as to exclude the free ingress and egress of fresh air; and no form of bedstead can offer so much comfort as to warmth.'

In the early Victorian era there was no change in the family bed, which still had four posts with a tester from which hung curtains to enclose the area of the bed. By the time of the Great Exhibition, however, the custom of sleeping in a fully curtained bed showed signs of decline (Fig. 14). By 1877 a writer in the *House Decoration* of that year has the following comment to make:

'Now that the venerable four-post bedstead is generally discarded, the mahogany half-tester has taken its place in most well-to-do houses. Until lately there has been a lurking prejudice against the brass-and-iron bedsteads, which are thought cold and mean-looking; and in order therefore to render them more attractive to his customers the manufacturer has begun to cover them with ormolu ornament, and to twist them out of the simplicity of form which, when only straight bars and rods are used, is one of their chief recommendations.'

The half-tester bed was one in which the tester top was extended over only half the length of the mattress; it was not upheld by posts, but was fixed to the framework forming the back of the bed. A clear example of this type of bed is illustrated in William Smee's catalogue (Fig. 1). In this design of bed, although the curtains hung at the sides, it was in most cases possible to enclose the sleeper by pulling the curtains round the half-tester. Further examples are illustrated in Figs. 14 and 65. The bed designed by John Dwyer (Fig. 228) is an exception to this and has side curtains only. Later, when brass bedsteads became the fashion, a half-tester was often retained, although it was not normally part of the structure of the bed but attached to the wall; the brass bedstead, which was quite a separate unit, was then placed under it. An example of this is illustrated in Fig. 226.

We can do no more than speculate as to why it was that the Victorians gave up sleeping in a space enclosed by curtains. Was it because they were the first of the English race to become fresh-air conscious? There is plenty of contemporary evidence to show that in Victorian times the doctors had changed their opinion as to the harmful effects of the night air. 'Medical men', so the writer in *Cassell's Guide* informs us, 'consider it the more healthy plan to sleep on beds with few draperies as possible. With a view to promote healthy slumbers, and yet have ornamental surroundings, furniture makers have again brought into general use the Arabian bedstead, in wood, iron, and brass, which they term "half-tester".'

It was the custom up to Victorian times for man and wife to share the 'family bed', which was a double bed of large dimensions. Nevertheless, the idea of twin beds had originated earlier; for instance, Sheraton in his *Drawing Book* shows a design of two beds enclosed by one tester upheld by posts with curtains hanging on all four sides. Sheraton describes the purpose of this bed to enable 'a nobleman or gentleman and his lady to sleep separately in hot weather'. But Sheraton's idea did not find much favour, for it was not until the end of Victoria's reign, and later, that twin beds became usual for double bedrooms.

Other furniture which the Victorians considered essential in the bedroom were the dressing table, washstand and wardrobe. The washstand was made either with one ewer or two, according to whether it was designed for a double or single bedroom (Figs. 226 and 227). The top of the washstand in the better quality pieces was made of marble, with a marble splashback to protect the wallpaper; there was often a hole cut in the marble to receive the basin. In the first half of Queen Victoria's reign the dressing table had a separate mirror (Fig. 229), which stood on the top in the 18th-century manner. Later the mirror became a fixture to the table, the glass being pivoted between two sets of drawers (Figs. 226, 227, 230, 232).

The dressing table, wardrobe and washstand were almost invariably designed *en suite*, with a similar design for leg mouldings, handles, etc. The wardrobe was made without wings for a single bedroom and with wings for a double room. In the last quarter of the 19th century it became usual to fit the centre wardrobe door with a panel of looking glass (Figs. 231 and 234). Prior to the general use of this looking glass panel, the independent cheval glass was a common piece of bedroom furniture.

The chest of drawers was another important article. It was usually made of a standard type with two fairly narrow width top drawers side by side and long drawers below. Another type of chest is illustrated in Fig. 235. This example of a high narrow chest is made *en suite* with the other furniture of the bedroom. It is an exceedingly useful and practical piece of furniture and had no counterpart in the 18th century.

The single bedroom would also contain at least one chair and the double bedroom two.

These chairs generally followed the style of the set of chairs in the drawing room. However, the detail would be much simpler and the woods used would be cheaper. Designs for six bedroom chairs are illustrated in Figs. 238 and 239.

In the larger bedroom there would often be a comfortable, upholstered chair placed near the fire. The occupant of the room, particularly if it were a lady, might well sit in front of the fire for a while before changing for dinner or at other times when she was in the bedroom. Coal fires were usual in bedrooms, for originally there was no other form of heating and with a large indoor staff of servants the problem of clearing grates and carrying coals did not arise. In the larger bedroom or man's dressing room there would be a low, upholstered chair without arms and a tall back; the seat would be about 8 or 9 inches from the ground. This chair would be used by a man when putting on and lacing up his shoes or boots, the low seat preventing uncomfortable bending.

The night convenience or night commode, as it was called in Victorian times, was very common in the first half of the period. The commode was generally camouflaged as a chest of drawers or fitted in the bedsteps, which in early Victorian times were often necessary; the four-posters at this time were high off the ground, and were made higher by the feather mattress, and it was, therefore, necessary to have steps to climb in and out with comfort. However, when the water closet became general, the night stool quickly became obsolete. The pedestal cupboard, which stood beside the bed and contained the chamber pot, was another usual piece of the bedroom suite.

A social change which is reflected in Victorian furniture is seen in the decline of the press-bed, which was camouflaged as a wardrobe or chest of drawers. It was made in far fewer numbers in Victorian times than in the 18th or first part of the 19th century. The press-bed of those days was often used to put up a guest who was reluctant to ride home, perhaps due to the darkness, the badness of the weather or who was maybe feeling the worse as a result of the entertaining that was traditional in the 19th century. It is possible that improved transport facilities and the more modest drinking of Victorian times made these temporary beds less essential.

As already described, it was necessary during the Victorian period for a room to be set apart in which men could indulge their taste for cigars and pipes. Robert Kerr, the architect and author of the *English Gentleman's House* (1863), has some interesting comments to make on the subject of smoking:

> 'The position selected for a Smoking-room is sometimes a species of prospect-chamber in a tower; sometimes a room upstairs to which a spacious balcony is attached; sometimes a chamber on the ground level, detached, or at least shut off from the Main House. In all cases of any importance the access ought to be as easy as may be from the Dining-room quarter; and if the room be situated on an upper floor it may even be well to have a small special stair to it.
>
> 'The prospect ought to be a pleasant one for the evening, and the aspect to be preferred will be Westward. A fireplace is necessary for winter; and complete ventilation is essential on the source of both health and cleanliness, so that a comparatively large ventilator in the ceiling will always be required. As regards prospect more particularly, it must be remem-

76

bered that such a room ought to have some sort of inducement attached to it apart from mere withdrawal; in other words, the smoker ought to be permitted to have some better excuse than the mere desire to smoke. For the same reason the room itself should be a good one, and well got up. In short, it ought to be a charming chatting-room with smoking allowed.'

Smoking rooms in the Victorian period were more often than not designed in the Turkish style. The reason for this was that better-class tobacco came from Turkey and, therefore, it seemed appropriate that the decoration and furnishing of the room should be in keeping with the country from which the tobacco was imported (Fig. 237).

The same thing occurred during the reign of Charles II when the drinking of China tea came in. The china and silver of the tea service, together with the japanned tea table, were all decorated in the Chinese taste. In the same way, in the 18th century, the book cases and furniture of libraries were often decorated with Gothic ornament because of the association between books and learning with the monasteries.

Judging from the frequent inclusion of furniture for the billiard room in trade catalogues in late Victorian times, this room must have been considered almost essential in the more well-to-do, middle-class home. Today unsightly additions can be seen on 18th-century houses where their Victorian and Edwardian owners had extended a room to accommodate a billiard table. One end of the billiard room was sometimes used as an additional sitting room, and also as a smoking room if the house was not large enough to have a special room for this purpose; in any event smoking would have been permitted in the billiard room.

In the 18th century the mural looking glass had a frame decorated with the ornament that was in fashion and which belonged to the different styles that followed each other throughout the century. Its usual place was between the windows, when it was called a pier-glass, or over the chimney-piece, when it was known as a chimney glass. In the Victorian period pier-glasses soon ceased to be made because of the popularity of the bay-window; one bay window in a room took the place of two or three sash windows which were set in one wall and divided by brick piers.

A large looking glass surmounting a gilt console table with a marble top was a favourite piece of furniture in the fashionable Victorian drawing room (Fig. 236). Such a looking glass was usually *en suite* with the chimney glass, and was often placed with its accompanying console table on the wall opposite the chimney-piece, in which position both glasses reflected each other, thereby causing the apparent size of the room to be increased. If of good quality, these large gilt-framed Victorian looking glasses were of carved wood and gilt; less expensive, the ornament was of carton pierre or papier mâché gilt. Several examples of a 'console glass in a carved and gilt frame' are illustrated in Smee's Catalogue. These looking glasses, which form part of the console table or the chimney-piece, were of upright proportions, but a glass of horizontal proportions—called an 'overmantel mirror'—was also made for the lesser rooms such as the parlour or bedroom.

The popularity of large looking glasses of the Victorian period can be traced to the improvement in glass manufacture, which dates from 1839, when James Chance invented 'patent plate', which was particularly suitable for windows of shops and houses and also looking glasses. One year later, in 1840, the old mercurial process for silvering mirrors was superseded by the chemical deposition of silver. As described in an earlier chapter, these improvements in glass making and silvering made the production of large looking glass plates possible and, in due course, reduced their cost, which brought them within the reach of the general public. By the Exhibition of 1862, we find looking glasses being incorporated in practically every kind of furniture, most particularly in sideboards.

The large gilt-framed looking glass went out of fashion some time in the 1870s, its place being taken by an overmantel designed with various shelves for the display of ornaments, surrounding a central mirror. The frame of this overmantel mirror, which was made of polished wood, was the work of the cabinet-maker. We learn of this change of fashion in the *Cabinet Maker* of 1890, in an article written on overmantels, where the writer mentions the elaborately enriched and gilded frames with 'super-abundance of meritorious splendour', which have happily become a thing of the past so far as better-class houses are concerned. The carved and polished overmantel mirror, with its numerous small shelves for *bric-à-brac,* was a feature of the Victorian reception room in the last thirty years of the reign. Examples of this can be seen in Figs. 51, 105, 123, 124 and 142.

CHAPTER FIVE

Techniques and Materials

IN THIS chapter machines, methods of construction and their effect on furniture production are considered. Also briefly discussed are some of the materials used in furniture making, which were often either new or adapted by the Victorians and gave their homes such a distinctive appearance.

With the exception of the turner's lathe, which dates back to the days of ancient Egypt, furniture craftsmen in the 18th century did not use wood-working machinery. There is, however, a considerable difference between the turner's lathe and the wood-working machinery that was introduced into furniture making in the 19th century. The lathe carried out work which it was not possible to do by hand; the wood-working machinery of the Victorians was in an entirely different category. It was invented in order to do processes more quickly and more cheaply, and in some cases more accurately than they could be done by the skilled craftsman with his hand tools. There were, however, some processes, such as wood carving, so difficult to imitate that the result, when done by machine, was much inferior to the hand-produced product.

The expanding population and the consequent increased demand for new furniture stimulated the ingenious minds of the Victorians. They solved the problem by inventing numerous machines, each one of which had as its prime object the lessening of the handwork necessary in furniture making. These machines, and the work they carried out, are briefly described later in this chapter.

It must not be supposed that the Victorian furniture maker was the first to consider cost. The 18th-century furniture maker, whether he was a craftsman working in a small provincial town or an eminent master cabinet-maker with premises in St Martin's Lane, fully appreciated that the cost of production was the all-important factor in running a successful business. The master craftsman, wherever he worked, was always striving to lower production costs to beat competition and to ensure larger profit margins. The idealistic picture of the 18th-century cabinet-maker, oblivious of economic factors, working like an inspired artist to create a masterpiece, is a complete misconception.

In the 18th century there was subdivision of labour in furniture making; a chair joiner made the frame of a chair, but did not carry out the carving or the turning, for this was the work of specialists—the carver and the turner. Craftsmen who specialised in the making of dining tables were not transferred to a workshop where the workmen were concentrating on furniture with drawers. A cabinet-maker was a specialist in veneered furniture; a joiner made frames of tables and chairs and, as the production of chairs was so great, the joiner who specialised in chair making was called a chair-maker.

Then there were the marquetry cutter and the fret cutter, who devoted their time to their own specialised activities. In the workshops of Chippendale or Vile, there was considerable subdivision of labour, because the master craftsman had found that he could get better quality work done more quickly and cheaply by the skilled craftsman who did one particular task. Specialisation was by no means invented by the Victorians, although they certainly extended it.

In order that this account of the subdivision of labour may be an overall one as regards furniture making in England, one must refer to the provincial craftsman who lived in a town where the demand for his work was comparatively small. Such a man, in order to make a living, had to turn his hand from one type of furniture to another; he and his journeymen, therefore, could not be specialists in one line alone. If he was commissioned to make a chair, for instance, he had no specialist carver standing by to do the carving, but had to undertake it himself. Such carving was, therefore, of a much lower standard than that of a skilled carver who did nothing else but work at his own craft.

Provincial furniture, made under such conditions, suffered in terms of quality when compared with the furniture made in a workshop where specialists were employed, each of whom confined his work to his own branch of the trade. It was for this simple economic reason and not, as is sometimes suggested today, for any lack or coarsening of taste in the provinces, that country-made furniture had its distinctive differences.

Besides this type of provincial craftsman, there was also another woodworker on an even lower grade. This was the man living and working in a small village community as a jack-of-all-trades. Since he was a woodworker he made all the local requirements in wood, whether they happened to be a bedstead, a barn door, a window frame, a table or a coffin. He was a combination of carpenter, joiner and cabinet-maker, and his work was necessarily of a rough-and-ready kind.

Apart from the subdivision of labour within one firm, there were subdivisions in the trade itself. In the 18th century there were certain firms which specialised in making certain articles. There were sideboard makers, wine-cooler makers, and dining-table makers; they worked wholesale, and sold their wares to cabinet-makers or shopkeepers who possessed a retail outlet for them. This type of division of labour was not so usual in the 18th century as it became in the 19th, when, in the London trade, there were innumerable subdivisions of skilled woodworkers. A list of these subdivisions includes 'wardrobe makers, pianoforte-case makers, dining-table makers, telegraphic-case makers, sideboard makers, glass-showcase makers, chiffonier makers, looking-glass-frame makers, mathematic-case makers, toilet and table makers, chest-of-drawer makers, etc.'

Once the need arose, wood-working machinery, actuated by steam, appears to have developed quickly and it had arrived at a standard of perfection by 1862, the year of the International Exhibition in London. According to a contemporary writer on the subject, 'improvements from 1862 to 1867 do not appear to have progressed at the same rate as from 1855 to 1862'. It would seem that Great Britain and Prussia were the two countries which developed the best wood-working machinery. The American and French machinery does not seem to have been able to stand up to the constant wear and the effect of the atmosphere—two factors which resulted in their machinery often going out of order and ultimately becoming useless. It would seem that the Americans and the French made their machinery to a more complex pattern than the English and Prussians, whose machines were simpler, as well as being more exact in their work.

The most important wood-working machines were for sawing, planing, moulding, morticing and tenoning, dovetailing and carving. There were also composite machines which combined the operations of sawing, planing, grooving and morticing and tenoning. Such machines, which could combine a number of intricate operations, were known in the trade as 'general joiners'.

The widespread demand for carving on furniture during the Victorian period meant inevitably that inventors turned their attention to the perfecting of wood-carving machinery. T. B. Jordan, inventor of the wood-carving machine illustrated in Fig. 246, pointed out in a paper read to the Royal Society of Arts in 1847 that 'the desire to carve by machinery has long existed, and several attempts have been made at different times, which have been attended with partial success'.

The machinery invented and patented by Jordan and his partners would appear, however, to have been the first completely successful specimen of its type, and his efforts were rewarded when he was presented with a gold medal by the Prince Consort. The machinery was extensively used for all types of wood carving, and the work in the House of Lords and the adjacent apartments was all undertaken by this process.

With Jordan's method innumerable copies could be made by mechanical cutters operated by steam power, all of them following the one master pattern, which was traced out by the workman in charge of the machinery. Jordan pointed out that 'the whole object of its application is to produce the work quickly and cheaply; and there is a point . . . at which the machine becomes more expensive than hand labour; and, therefore, it is a matter of commercial calculation how far it is desirable to finish on the machine, and when to deliver it into the hands of the workmen'. An improved version of Jordan's original model was even able to undertake such difficult tasks as undercut carving—something that had never previously been within the scope of the mechanical carver.

'Steel carving' was the name given to another method introduced into England in about 1870 by the Ornamental Wood Company of Bridgeport, Connecticut, U.S.A. This type of carving was produced by steel dies operated under pressure, the wood being roughly shaped to the form required in advance, and then being placed under the die. The defect in this work, which prevented it being used on the best-quality furniture, was that the carving showed the end and not the long grain of the wood.

Bois Durci is a name given to imitation ebony carvings of French manufacture, which were introduced into England. Carvings of this type were used for ornamenting the ebonised cabinets for which there was so great a vogue in France. These ornaments were in the form of medallions, Grecian heads, rosettes and paterae. Unlike the American pressed steel carvings, they were made out of sawdust, principally rosewood, which had been ground into a fine powder. This fine sawdust was mixed with a quantity of animal blood and water, and then subjected to a heat process. During the heat treatment the albumen in the blood became amalgamated with the sawdust, producing a composite substance which could then be subjected to steel die-stamping.

The whole complex process, which was described in a paper read to a French technical association, produced pseudo-ebony ornaments which still came out at about one-third of the cost of the genuine carved ornament. This is evidence of the degree to which manufacturers would go in order to reduce the cost of production for their elaborate furniture.

The circular saw, it is said, first came into use at the end of the 18th century. In Victorian times it was of considerable importance. The cheap furniture makers could not have worked at the price they did if they had not used this saw, which could square up, mitre, rabbet, etc.; and the work was ready to be put together for it cut very cleanly and accurately. The circular saw was particularly useful in making carcases, for, by rabbeting the ends which were then nailed together, it did away with dovetailing.

Wood sawn by the circular saw has an arc visible on the rough surface, where the saw has cut. The presence of these circular marks on wood indicates that the furniture could not have been made prior to the late 18th century. In Victorian reproduction work—as well as in fakes—these circular saw marks are conclusive evidence of the period in which the piece was made. These marks, however, can generally be seen only on the carcase, because the rest of the wood, such as the sides and drawer linings, would be planed; in high-quality furniture the carcase wood also was planed.

Next to the circular saw the fret saw was the most useful tool of the cabinet-maker; it was on a stand with treadle and fly-wheel—and similar in most respects to the circular saw. Ornamental fret panels, backed by silk, were a feature of Victorian furniture.

The way in which a drawer is constructed affects its running and is evidence of the quality of the workmanship. Nothing denotes a badly made piece of furniture more quickly than ill-fitting drawers. There are two types of dovetailing to drawers, one being known as common dovetailing and the other as lap dovetailing. In common dovetailing the pins pass right through the drawer front. This is the strongest and easiest to make, and consequently also the cheapest. The difference between lap dovetailing and common is that in the former the dovetail does not penetrate the drawer front, but is stopped by a lap cut in the drawer front. This latter method is the best and correct method for drawer construction. An example is shown in Fig. 138.

The typical Victorian drawer construction was one in which the drawer bottom was let into a grooved drawer slip, which was either pinned or glued on to the drawer side. The drawer front was also grooved to take the bottom board. At the back of the drawer the bottom board was loose and extended beyond the drawer back. Sometimes it was screwed to the back lining, but in order to let the bottom have some flexibility the screw was normally fixed in an elongated hole, so that it did not hold the bottom down and cause it to split if the wood shrank (Fig. 139). Victorian drawers are distinguished by the quarter round top of the drawer slip, which is seen between the drawer side and the drawer bottom.

Although Bruce Talbert expressed his dislike of glue—for he was a lover of good joinery work (where the joints fitted each other so well that glue was unnecessary)—the fact remains that in the craft of the cabinet-maker glue is essential. To the layman one glue may seem to be very like another, but the skilled cabinet-maker needed a more precise knowledge. Different woods have different strengths and require a different thickness and type of glue. Generally speaking, for softwoods such as pine and soft mahogany, the glue should be thin. Hardwoods require a thicker consistency. Synthetic glues are used today, but in Victorian times all glues had to be made up out of animal or fish substances. Russian and Italian glues were considered good and were both of a light colour. They were extracted from skins and parings of hide and boiled to a jelly. London glue, on the other hand, was made by boiling animal tissues, such as muscles, cartilages, tendons and bones, hoofs and hides. Richard Bitmead, author of the *London Cabinet-Maker's Guide,* remarks that the best sort made in England was Salisbury glue.

The working of mouldings by hand was a good test of the skill of the cabinet-maker. The mouldings were planed to the shape required, and one of the most important things was to ensure that the planes were perfectly sharpened. If they were not, the mouldings would not be true to section. The quality of their arrises and the roundness of their members is a particularly pleasant feature and one which adds to the enjoyment of the man who knows and appreciates a well-formed moulding when he sees it.

In the Victorian period there were three principal types of mouldings—the Roman, the Grecian and the Gothic. Each moulding had its own particular name, such as ovolo, carvetto, sima recta (usually called ogee), sima reversa, and the torus or half-round. When a half-round is very small with a square on each side, it is called an astragal moulding, and when a half-round is worked on the edge of a board it is called a bead. Several beads used together are called reeds. The scotia, a hollow moulding, is the reverse of the torus. The Greek mouldings, although of the same character as the Roman, have different curves which, to a knowledgeable eye, are immediately recognisable.

Mouldings were also cut by machine during the Victorian period. A rotary moulding cutter, called the *Toupie,* was a particularly valuable tool. It worked quickly and the cutting of the wood was very clean; and any number of small members could be introduced into one section of a moulding. This was of immense advantage in certain types of work. For Gothic or Mediaeval mouldings, this machine was said to be invaluable, since more chamfering could be done with it in one hour than could be done by hand in a whole day.

Marquetry furniture was particularly fashionable in the mid-Victorian period. The majority was in the form of veneer of Colonial woods, and examples of floral design of the highest quality were made by firms such as Jackson and Graham and Holland & Son; for examples of marquetry by the latter see Figs. 167, 178, 240 and 241.

In the early Victorian period marquetry furniture was imported from France, but in the course of time foreign workmen—specialists, skilled in Buhl and marquetry cutting—established themselves in London and worked for the cabinet trade. By the 1870s it is said that the English marquetry cutters were able to compete with any of the continental firms. After the Franco-Prussian war many orders for marquetry work were diverted to London which previously would have gone to Paris. Some of the foremost London firms like Jackson and Graham employed their own marquetry cutters.

The tool required in the cutting of marquetry is a fret saw and frame. The saws used are as thin as horsehair. A marquetry cutter, who designed his own work, needed to be a good draughtsman as well as to have an understanding of the harmony of coloured woods, and an ability to arrange them artistically.

The following was the usual procedure: the design was drawn out in full on oil or tracing paper and then all the lines were pricked out with tiny pin holes at very close intervals; then it was decided what wood was to be used in each section of the marquetry and the tracing was marked accordingly. The drawing was then placed over the appropriate piece of wood and a duster, known as a pounce, containing a fine powder (often asphalt dust) was tapped up and down on the drawing: the powder penetrated the tiny holes and left an outline on the wood underneath. It was then lightly heated and it was a property of the dust that it then became sticky and adhered to the wood. This enabled the appropriate pieces of wood to be accurately cut out; the process was repeated until all parts were cut.

To produce fine marquetry everything depended on the craftsman's skill in using the saw. When the sawing of the various coloured veneers had been completed, the shading of the flowers, leaves, etc. was accomplished by the use of a tray filled with dry clean sand to a depth of about two inches. The tray was heated on a stove, and when the sand became hot the portions of the marquetry veneer which required shading were inserted into it. The part that came out darkest was that which was buried the deepest, and the shade gradually lightened as the veneer protruded from the sand.

After shading, the marquetry cutter then assembled the pieces, as in a jig-saw puzzle, and pasted a piece of clean paper on the side to be displayed, thus holding all the pieces firm; he then prepared the reverse side for glueing and in this state it was sent off to the cabinet-maker. The cabinet-maker glued the reverse side and put it into the required position with clamps. After it was firmly stuck in position, the cabinet-maker finished the rest of the furniture, then cleaned the paper off the surface of the marquetry and the piece was ready for polishing.

Polishing was an exceedingly important part of furniture production and various methods were used in the Victorian era, the principal ones being oil polish, wax polish and french polish. A Victorian recipe for oil polish was one quart of cold-drawn linseed oil to be simmered (not boiled) for ten minutes, and strained through flannel. One-eighth part of spirits of turpentine was then added. The polish was applied daily with soft linen rags and rubbed off lightly. Each time the oil was applied, the surface was previously washed with cold water to remove any dirt or dust. This method of polishing was particularly useful for dining-table tops and in about six weeks produced a surface so durable as to resist boiling water or hot dishes, and which was like a looking glass for brilliance.

In the case of wax polish, the composition was made of eight parts of beeswax, two parts resin and a half part of Venetian turpentine, which was heated over a slow fire. When completely melted, it was poured into a large stoneware pot and while still warm six parts rectified turpentine were stirred into it. After twenty-four hours it would have assumed the consistency of soft butter and be ready for use. It was applied with a woollen rag and rubbed over the surface of the work, at first gently and then more strongly. After the polish had been uniformly laid, it was then rubbed lightly and quickly with fresh, clean rag to produce a gloss; this polish could be applied with ease and could be used by an inexperienced person. In the case of furniture designed in the Mediaeval and Old English style wax polish was much preferred to french polish for it was considered to be more in keeping with the character of the woodwork of the Middle Ages.

Before the introduction of french polish, oil or wax polish was used for chairs, tables and cabinet ware. French polish was, as its name indicates, the invention of French cabinet-makers. It was first introduced into England in the first quarter of the 19th century. To make use of french polish required a special skill, and it is said that the early french polishers worked in a shop by themselves, with closed doors, in order to preserve the secrets of this new method. After the widespread adoption of french polish, the craft of polishing for the first time became a separate branch of the furniture trade. Previously polishing had always been undertaken by the cabinet-makers themselves.

The first process in french polishing was to 'fill in'. This consisted of rubbing into the pores of the wood a mixture of Russian tallow and plaster of Paris, which had been previously heated and mixed together. After this had been rubbed in thoroughly, the surface was cleaned of all the surplus with scrapers and then rubbed clean with soft old rag. In the case of white and light-coloured woods some polishers used plaster of Paris and methylated spirits for filling in the grain. For polishing pine a coat of clear size was first laid in to counteract the suction of the soft absorbent wood.

A Victorian recipe for french polish reads as follows: '1 pint methylated spirit; 4 oz. shellac; ¼ oz. sandarach.' For cheap work a polish called 'patent glaze' was used. This was known to the Victorian furniture trade under various names, such as Slake, Slick, Finish and Telegraph, and was made of 1 oz. mastic, 5 oz. benzoin, and 5 gills spirit.

Reducing costs in order to capture as much as possible of the market which required cheap furniture was always the aim of the majority of manufacturers. Richard Bitmead in 1873 wrote in his *London Cabinet-Maker's Guide* that 'the demand everywhere is for quantity and cheapness, which renders it necessary that workmen should be acquainted with every method of constructing work in the quickest and easiest manner possible, so as to be able to compete with cheap trade-workers and foreign importations'.

The author then goes on to explain that with cheap work the carcase-ends were dowelled into the plinth and frieze, which were part of the main carcase. Bitmead also gives a detailed description of a French method of making doors and he adds that 'more than double the quantity of doors can be made in this way, in a given time, than could be done by morticing and tenoning, and for cheap work the strength and durability are greater than might be imagined'.

In this form of cheap work, marquetry was stamped out, and not sawn and cut; and knife-cut veneers were always used. The cornices of cabinets were blocked to the top of the frieze, instead of being made separately. After the carcase had been put together, the inside was lined—usually with velvet—thus hiding all the defects in the carcase wood. After the polishing was done a few brass ornaments were fixed to the pilasters. 'This method of construction is applied by the continental cabinet-makers to sideboards, book cases and small carcases, and a saving is effected both in materials and in time, for first, a much thinner carcase bottom is used; secondly, no carcase top is required; and thirdly, the carcase can be put together in less than half the time that it could be by dovetailing after the English system; but of course the same durability is not obtained.'

Bitmead also writes about the framing of tables by the French and German cabinet-makers which, he says, 'differs considerably from the substantial manner in which they are put together in most English shops, viz., by mortices and double tenons'.

An interesting comment is that cheap tables were also made in this manner 'by the little trade-masters who supply the pretenders at cabinet-making—the puffing linen-drapery shops and the furniture bazaars; indeed, the whole of the furniture at these places is made in the same flimsy manner, to sell cheap'.

The following information is also of interest, for it shows how cheap and shoddy was the cabinet-ware at the lower end of the Victorian furniture trade:

'If the furniture sold at these places were made as well as that which is sold by respectable manufacturers, and which can be depended upon to wear well for years, the price would be about the same, as the whole of the materials are purchased from the same dealers; the only difference is that the cheap workers buy the cheapest and commonest articles—those, in fact, which the makers of good furniture refuse to purchase. Without doubt cheap cabinet work can only be made by being put together in an inferior manner, with less work, and as a consequence less wages to pay, and by the use of common materials. But, as a rule, workmen who are accustomed to make the common class of work, known as "trade work", generally prefer to keep in that line. Although the price paid for making an article in the best shops of the West End is about double what is paid for the same thing in the "trade work" shops, the cheap workers can often earn more money than the West End workmen, who are obliged to put every part of their work together in a sound and workmanlike manner, which is more satisfying to a good workman, and more creditable to an employer. But it is not so with the "cut and run" work which is made for the linen-drapery establishments. These places will encourage all sorts of deceptions, so long as the work is cheap and a good profit can be made out of it.'

Cheap carved oak furniture was also imported from Belgium. The carving was good, but the carcase construction was very inferior. These imports consisted mostly of book cases, cabinets and sideboards, the decoration being after the Gothic or the Elizabethan styles. The construction was done in the cheapest possible way, for the carcase ends and the doors had no mortices. 'The stiles are ploughed rather deep (about five-eighths), and a stub-tenon is made on the ends of the rails to fit the plough groove and then glued together.' Dovetailing did not exist in any of this furniture. The drawers, plinths and friezes were all glued together and the wood was not planed but left rough.

The London Cabinet-Maker's Guide also records that 'the cheap trade houses which are now springing up in every town, trying to supplant the establishments which make good honest work, also make their work in this common manner'.

The Victorians revived and often extended the use of various materials both for making and decorating furniture. One such was the type of inlay work called Buhl, which became extremely popular in the mid-Victorian period; another was papier mâché, which was used extensively for trays and smaller pieces of furniture, and more rarely for larger pieces. Buhl work came to England from France and was frequently made by Frenchmen working in this country.

Victorian Buhl work was an inlay of brass, usually with a red or green tortoiseshell backing; in cheaper work turtle shell was more often used. Buhl was used particularly for commodes (Figs. 242 and 243) and china cabinets. It was said that cabinet-makers were very careful in their selection of the workmen to whom they entrusted this kind of work, for an inexperienced and poor craftsman could easily ruin expensive materials.

Buhl work, like marquetry, was cut with a fine saw. After it had been veneered on to the surface, considerable trouble and expense were taken to present a perfectly smooth face. This was done with a large, flat file and pumice stone; then, once it had been ground, it was rubbed with linseed oil and finished off with 'fine flor' and emery paper. This treatment resulted in a surface that was perfectly smooth and level. In the best quality work the brass parts of the design were then engraved; when the engraver had finished his work, the piece of furniture was ready for polishing.

Ormolu mounts were much used on Buhl and other Victorian furniture. Ormolu is the French name for a metal alloy composed of 58% copper and 42% brass. This alloy is well-adapted for mercurial or water gilding, in which process the exposed surfaces of the mount are brushed with gold. In furniture, where this type of mount would have been too expensive, an imitation was made by lacquering brass. This in time discolours through exposure to the atmosphere—a defect which, of course, does not apply to the more costly process. The mounts are fixed by fine brass pins or screws, inconspicuously placed. Metal mounts and decoration can be seen on several of the pieces illustrated; two detailed photographs are shown in Figs. 244 and 245.

Chairs with wrought-iron frames made by the blacksmith date back to the 15th century. These frames were afterwards often covered in rich materials and trimmings. In the 18th century garden chairs were made in this way and painted. However, not until the Victorians used cast-iron was there any considerable production in this material.

Apart from chairs and beds, sideboards and tables were made with their wooden tops supported on cast-iron feet or wall brackets; elaborate examples of cast-iron hat and coat stands were also popular.

J. C. Loudon in his *Encyclopaedia* states that, as lobby chairs were seldom moved, they may be made with cast-iron frames. The chair Loudon illustrates is of cast-iron suitable for a porch, and he describes the design as 'Etruscan', and says that it can be cast in two pieces. Loudon also illustrates a chair of a plain functional design with tubular legs. Such chairs, which were designed by an architect named Mallet, were for use in the kitchen. Unlike the 'Etruscan' chair, these were 'exceedingly light' and were the ancestors of the modern tubular framed chair. Cast-iron was always cheaper than wood, even if only a small number of a certain design were required. The 'Etruscan' and the kitchen chair are illustrated in Figs. 247 and 248.

Loudon suggested that cast-iron chairs should be painted in imitation of oak, and gave a description of how the painting should be carried out. As in every other age, but perhaps more particularly in the Victorian, the introduction of something new had its critics. Iron furniture was no exception, and Welby Pugin had the following pertinent comment to make:

> 'Cast-iron is a deception; it is seldom or never left as iron. It is disguised by paint, either as stone, wood or marble. This is a mere trick ... Cheap deceptions of magnificence encourage persons to assume a semblance of decoration far beyond either their means or their station, and it is to this cause we may assign all that mockery of splendour which pervades even the dealings of the lower classes of society. Glaring, showy and meretricious ornament was never so much in vogue as at present; it disgraces every branch of our art and manufactures, and the correction of it should be an earnest consideration with every person who desires to see the real principles of art restored.'

The graining and painting of cast-iron to look like wood was the type of deceit that the

Victorians were more proud of—in general—than ashamed. Throughout the 17th and 18th centuries, of course, the graining of a poor quality wood to make it represent a better one had been commonly done.

Composition and papier mâché were not new to the Victorians, although they greatly extended their use. Composition was much used in the 1760s when ornament in low relief was an essential feature of the neo-classic style. The Adam brothers, in order to overcome the high cost of so much carved work, which their favoured style required, used patent stucco for the production of ornament in low relief. This, when cast in moulds and glued on to the wood background and painted, had all the appearance of carving. Similar composition 'ornaments' were soon generally adopted by the building trade, and by carvers and gilders, for the decoration which had previously been left entirely to the carver.

James Thorp, for instance, in 1783 mentions the 'ornaments' which could be made from 'Thorp's Composition', and he writes of them as follows: 'Any ornament, contained in these Designs, will be executed of Composition fifty per cent cheaper than Wood Carvings, though in many respects they are equal in goodness.' This composition was a mixture of whiting and glue.

Although a detailed study of composition belongs more to a work on decoration, it must be realised that considerable use was made of it in Victorian times for looking glass and picture frames as well as for decorating gilt or painted furniture. When the ornament was in high relief or in the round, as in the cresting of a looking glass, it was mounted on wire.

A different method of imitating carving was by the use of papier mâché. This material, which appears to have originated in Persia and the East, was being widely used by the mid-18th century for decorative ornaments, as well as for large-scale decoration on walls and ceilings. The supplement for *Chambers's Encyclopaedia*, 1753, tells us that 'Paper, besides its common uses, may be made into frames for pictures, fine embossed work and other parts of furniture'. An important manufacturer of this period was Thomas Bromwich, who was in business as a leather gilder about 1740. Nearly all the principal manufacturers of paper hangings and, subsequently, of papier mâché, were originally associated with the making of leather hangings and their decoration. It may be reasonably assumed that, as paper in one form or another was more and more employed for decoration, so the craft of the leather gilder declined and the manufacturers and artisans associated with this work transferred their attentions to wall-paper and papier mâché ornament. We learn that in 1765 Thomas Bromwich was paid £54 12s. od. by James West, the owner of Alscot Park, Warwickshire, 'for ornamenting the Drawing-Room Ceiling with Rich Gothick Papier Mâché ornaments'. The great advantage of papier mâché for such ornamentation was that the articles concerned could be manufactured in London and transported anywhere in the country ready for application—thus obviating the presence of plasterers working in a country gentleman's home, as well as being considerably less expensive.

The material was also widely used for making looking glass frames in the middle decades of the 18th century. Looking glasses were extremely popular at this time and the elaborate carving of a frame by hand was not only expensive, but necessitated a skilled carver. A mould from which fifty or more frames could be produced was clearly a great saving in cost. Such looking glass frames would not show any undercutting in the ornament, but when they were gilded they were difficult to distinguish from carved wood frames. That they are not wood is obvious from their weight, and when the frame is looked at from the back it will be seen to be hollow, due to the paper pulp having shrunk when fully dried out.

Although papier mâché is the French term for pulped paper, the 19th-century English product which is normally recognised under this name was made by a different technique. It was formed by paper laid in sheets and pasted together over a mould; it was then stoved to render it durable. This technique of making papier mâché in sheet paper is said to have been invented by Henry Clay in 1772, at which time he took out a patent for this particular process.

Clay was strict in making the distinction between his product and the true papier mâché of other manufacturers, where the paper was used in a pulped state. 'Paper ware' was the term that Clay applied to the productions of his factory, and for some fifty or sixty years this distinction was maintained. His successors, however, Messrs Jennens and Bettridge, possibly feeling that the term suggested a low grade article, marketed their similar products as 'papier mâché'. Other manufacturers followed suit, and from this has arisen a confusion in the public mind—the articles which should strictly be referred to as 'paper ware' being indiscriminately termed 'papier mâché'.

A contemporary account of Clay's Birmingham manufactory is given by Edward Clarke in his tour of England and Wales in 1791:

'A number of sheets of paper are pasted together and dried; they are then carried into a room, resembling a little timber-yard, contiguous to which is a very large workshop: cabinet-makers form every article as it is required, sawing it out of paper and planing it with the greatest exactness. It is then japanned and polished, and this is always done with the hand, which gives a more exquisite lustre to steel or paper work than can be communicated by any other means.'

During the Victorian period the production of papier mâché became an important trade, for the articles could be mass-produced at small cost, and after the surface had been decorated with japanning, the finished product looked worth a great deal more than its actual cost. Clay sold a single tea tray for £5 8s. 9d., on which sale it is said he made a profit of £3 8s. 2d. Japanning and papier mâché were closely allied; papier mâché was a new and improved material for the japanners to use and considerably better than the various metals that they had used formerly. The tea tray was the most important item in both trades—the japanned tin tea tray being superseded by the japanned papier mâché tea tray.

The two distinct methods of manufacturing papier mâché (during the 19th century) are summarised in the *Illustrated Catalogue of the Great Exhibition of 1851*. The first is by pasting paper in sheets upon models (Clay's process), the second by pressing in dies the pulp of paper. 'The former produces the best quality, and the latter the least expensive and inferior kinds.'

The making of papier mâché furniture was divided between the production of the actual ware and the decoration of its surface by the japanner. The large manufacturer carried out both processes, but there were many more smaller firms who did the japanning only, buying the plain undecorated ware—known in the trade as 'blanks'—from the papier mâché manufacturer.

The home of the papier mâché trade was Birmingham, where Clay's first factory had been established, and Wolverhampton. Jennens and Bettridge were the most important Birmingham firm during the Victorian era, and apart from the normal activities of the papier mâché trade they were among the first to specialise in papier mâché furniture. This, in itself, was not a new idea, for Clay had also made furniture out of the material; a sedan chair, which he gave to Queen Caroline, had panels of papier mâché.

Jennens and Bettridge, however, extended the range of papier mâché furniture-making (Fig. 249). At the Crystal Palace they exhibited, among other articles, a number of papier mâché chairs. Tables were also made by this firm, a solid rod being fixed inside the central pillar to take the weight. Even cabinets and book cases were made in the material—as well as pianofortes and bedsteads, the latter having an iron frame inside the papier mâché exterior. Some examples of papier mâché furniture are illustrated in Figs. 250–260.

Charles F. Bielefeld was another manufacturer; his factory was at 15, Wellington Street North, Strand. He issued in 1850 a large illustrated catalogue of 'Ornaments applicable to the Decoration of Interior Domestic and Private Buildings'. The Grocers' Hall, the British Museum, the State Drawing Rooms at Dublin Castle, and the Corn Exchange were among the many important buildings where Bielefeld's papier mâché ornaments were used.

Bielefeld was producing real papier mâché or paper pulp ornaments and not the 'paper ware' of Jennens and Bettridge and other manufacturers of furniture and decorative objects.

Papier mâché had its critics and one of them, Richard Redgrave, in his *Supplementary Report on Design at the Great Exhibition*, writes: 'There is no apparent reason why this material should not be used for chairs, couches, tables or cradles; but the art of designing for it is not yet attained: as the material possesses peculiar properties of strength and lightness, without needing any framing it should be considered purely for itself, and the designer must forget all other constructive forms. As to its ornamentation, the sooner it has a thorough revision the better, since at present it is a mass of barbarous splendour that offends the eye and quarrels with every other kind of manufacture with which it comes in contact. The simple lacquered work of India may afford an example for the ornamentation of papier mâché.'

The decorative processes employed in the japanning of papier mâché ware were many and varied. Gold in the form of gold leaf or gold powder was the chief ingredient. Where cheapness was the over-riding consideration, the 'gold' was an alloy composed of metals such as copper, brass, zinc and silver. The enrichment of the floral decoration or painted scene by the use of these metals gave unusual and dramatic effects. Joseph Booth, an artist employed by Jennens and Bettridge, was among the first to treat the new material seriously. He executed imitations of Japanese and Chinese work with extreme delicacy, using gold size and whitening to produce the elevated sections of his designs.

In 1825 George Souter, another employee of Jennens and Bettridge, introduced pearl-shell inlaying. The method was that very thin pearl shell was inlaid on the piece and then a decoration or design was painted on to the shell with varnish, which acted as a protective coat. When this had dried, acid was applied and the unprotected portions of the shell were eaten away leaving the varnished decoration unharmed. A pretty and effective example of this technique can be seen in Fig. 250, where a bird and a butterfly amidst flowers are portrayed in two circles on either side of the mirror. A chess board using the same method can be seen on the table in Fig. 255.

Other decorative processes were later applied to papier mâché articles; one such was geminlaying, which consisted in substituting for the pearl-shell, coloured glass stones or 'paste'. Another material was aluminium in the form of a powder, which was found to be of the greatest value for the painting of picturesque scenes in the romantic vogue.

Yet another method of decoration was to incorporate a coloured print, which would be stuck onto a smooth surface of the piece and then varnished over. An example of this can be seen in the firescreen illustrated in Fig. 258. A variation of this was the incorporation of a painted board or panel; these panels were sometimes specially imported from abroad or cut out from an earlier piece of decoration; an example of the incorporation of a panel can be seen in the back of a chair in Fig. 253. Floral decoration became increasingly popular as the century advanced (Figs. 256 and 259). One of the artists who made a speciality of this type of work was George Neville of Birmingham.

Although many papier mâché articles—such as tea and pen trays, boxes, small tables and chairs—still survive, much of the furniture made from, or embodying, this material has long since disappeared. An example of a larger piece of furniture of conventional construction, but incorporating papier mâché panels, is illustrated in Fig. 260. The framework is constructed in wood in the normal way and only the four door panels are made of papier mâché.

We learn that in 1866, so great was the volume of trade, that 'besides the ordinary articles for house-consumption, large quantities of panels for steamboat cabins, dining-room furniture, etc. are made for the export trade to Canada, North and South America, Russia, Spain, etc., besides an immense variety of large pieces of household furniture, wardrobes, loo and other tables, dressing-tables, sofas and couches, decorated to suit the taste or the want of taste of purchasers in the countries to which they are exported. . . . The style of ornamentation adopted in these articles has, there can be little question, materially injured the trade by fostering a taste for exuberant decoration, opposed to all true principles of ornamental art'.

Although household furniture such as chairs, tripod tables, looking glasses and many other pieces were all made of papier mâché, the main article of the trade was the tea tray. These had the merit of being able to present a surface admirably suited for the portrayal of flowers, birds, cathedrals, moonlight landscapes, and many other subjects.

Good quality papier mâché work would seem to have reached its peak in about the middle of the century. A list given by G. Dickinson in his book *English Papier Mâché* (1925) reveals the remarkable number of patents which were taken out between 1772, when Clay obtained his first patent, and 1864, when Bettridge patented the application of aluminium to the material. From its humble beginnings papier mâché had expanded in nearly a century to a thriving industry.

The lack of taste exhibited by many of the later manufacturers in the 1860s and 1870s, when mass-production was flooding the market, caused a reversal of public taste, and by the 1880s papier mâché had gone out of favour.

Carton pierre was a substance analogous to papier mâché. It was a French invention used extensively in England during the 19th century, particularly by the firm of George Jackson & Sons, of Rathbone Place, London, for the purpose of architectural decoration applied to ceilings, walls and woodwork. For an accurate definition of carton pierre we must refer to G. W. Yapp's *Furniture, Upholstery and Household Decoration* (1878):

'Carton pierre ornaments are made of paper pulp mixed with whiting and glue, cast in plaster moulds, and dried gradually in a hot room. It is admirably adapted for large decorations on account of its lightness and durability.'

George Jackson's carton pierre was an improvement over the French material, it was said, because 'they had overcome the extreme fragility and susceptibility to moisture'. It had little strength and was therefore used only when applied as decoration to a base of either plaster or wood. Jacksons issued a catalogue showing to what extent they had used carton pierre ornament, which ranged in style from the Middle Ages up to the Greek revival. They specialised particularly in ceilings and the cornices and enrichment of panel mouldings. When seen at a distance, carton pierre decoration, cast in a mould and painted, was difficult to distinguish from carved wood. One had to put the point of a penknife into it and if hard it was carton pierre, and if soft it was wood.

Bentwood furniture was one of the Victorians' most happy inventions. Chairs and seats, with frames made of beech and bent to any required shape by heat and steam treatment, were an invention of Messrs Thonet of Vienna (Figs. 261 and 262). This firm also had an establishment in London and its products were sold here in great quantities. It is said, in fact, that by 1891 seven million bentwood chairs had so far been produced by the Viennese factory.

The first bentwood chairs were made in the 1830s, but during the last half of the 19th century they became widely popular and sold in great quantities throughout England. The legs, arms and backs of such chairs were curved in pleasing and graceful designs, and apart from this the chairs were extremely comfortable in use.

The bentwood chair was the forerunner of the tubular steel chair of modern times, but whereas the modern chair has leather upholstery, the Thonet bentwood chairs were completed in cane. The remarkable thing at the time about this furniture was its combination of lightness with strength, as well as the use of mass-production techniques, which enabled such chairs to be marketed at a low cost.

Much of the difference between the furnishings of the 18th- and early 19th-century house and its counterpart in the Victorian era can be understood by making a comparison of the upholstered furniture of the two periods. In the former age, the consideration of elegance and beauty was the main factor in decorating and furnishing the home, even if this meant some consequent sacrifice of comfort. As the grand and stately life of the 18th century gave way in Victorian times to a way of living which valued opulence and luxury more, so upholstered furniture changed.

The 18th century saw the production of graceful chairs and sofas, in which the upholsterer played a major part. The seats and curved backs, and sometimes the arms, were completely covered and it was only the visible parts, generally the legs, that were of polished wood. The elegance of these pieces lay mainly in the upholstery, for the craftsman's art was to endow a chair or sofa with a graceful form by the way in which he stuffed and shaped the upholstered parts. The framework of these pieces was made of beech, the foundation of webbing, and the stuffing of horsehair. The latter was shaped and curved in the most skilled manner, and covered with canvas, which in its turn was covered by the upholstery material of silk or damask. A chair or sofa would be trimmed along its edges by close-nailing with brass-headed nails, which gave a neat finish. Brass nailing had been used for fixing coverings to upholstered chairs as far back as the 15th century.

Bodily comfort was not lost sight of in this upholstered furniture of the 18th century, although, unlike in later times, it was not permitted to interfere over much with the lines of the piece. What comfort was allowed was attained by a soft seat and resilient back. The back was of webbing and horsehair, and the seat—in a sofa or winged-back chair—was formed by a covered platform upheld by webbing upon which was placed a loose squab stuffed with feathers. On the other hand, armchairs, which were not made with so great a view to comfort as the wing chair, had the seats of webbing and horsehair. These 18th-century chairs and sofas never had a bloated or blown up appearance, for the upholstery was neat, with clean-cut lines.

This 18th-century line continued into the 19th century. In the 1830s some restraint remained in the outline and shape of upholstered furniture, and this can be seen from the sofas and chair illustrated in Figs. 263, 264 and 269.

With the invention of springs, which were used to give additional resiliency to the backs and seats, the shape of easy chairs and sofas became much more flamboyant. The squab was done away with and spiral springs, which were hidden with a deep seat rail, took its place. By 1833 springs for backs and seats were being made in Birmingham by the hundredweight for the use of upholsterers, a fact which we know from Loudon's *Encyclopaedia*, published in that year.

Brass nailing went out of fashion in the Regency period, and machine-made gimp began to be used for Victorian furniture to hide the tacks which secured the material to the frame. In the first part of the Victorian period, chairs and sofas showed their polished mahogany or rosewood legs and arms, and the upholstered back of a sofa would often be enclosed by a polished wood frame. Easy chairs had concave upholstered backs, with the arm-supports and legs shaped and carved. Examples of this style can be seen in Figs. 265 and 266. A variety of upholstered chairs and a sofa can be seen in the illustration of Queen Victoria's retiring room at the Crystal Palace (Fig. 276); no doubt this furniture was the height of fashion in 1851. A chair, identical to the one shown in the foreground in the Queen's retiring room, is illustrated in Fig. 270. The tendency was for upholstery to become more curved and inflated and, in consequence, upholstered furniture became larger and took up more space in a room.

A new fashion, which became extremely popular in upholstered furniture in the first half of the Victorian period, was for all chairs and couches to have their upholstery fixed by deeply sunk buttons, which had the effect of emphasising the curves and thickness of the upholstery. This deep buttoning was particularly popular with the general furniture trade, and Story's of London Wall were showing it on nearly all the upholstered furniture illustrated in their catalogue issued about 1865. Some examples from this catalogue are in Figs. 68 and 70. Buttoning appears to have come in during the second decade of the 19th century, for a chair so covered is illustrated in *Ackerman's Depository*, the plate being dated 1813.

Generally the backs of the early and mid-Victorian sofas were deeply curved and shaped, although this was not always the case. An exception can be seen in the middle ground of the Furniture Court at the Great Exhibition (Fig. 9); apart from the heavily carved arm supports, this sofa has a decidedly 20th-century appearance.

Large easy chairs and also sofas were often upholstered in Oriental carpet (Fig. 278). In France these large chairs were called 'confortables'. The back, the arms and the seat were all sprung and nothing was now to be seen in the way of the frame, because the deep fringe which came to the ground hid the small, low feet. In the words of Henry Havard in his *Dictionnaire de l'Ameublement et de la Décoration* (circa 1878), it was *'La victoire de la garniture sur le bois'*—'The victory of the covering over the wood'.

The use of springs and the covering of the entire frame of the upholstered chair and couch were the two most important innovations that took place in the upholsterer's craft in the second and third quarters of the 19th century. Once the sofa and easy chair with a frame hidden in the upholstery came into fashion in England, its popularity grew and has continued to the present time. By 1878 Mrs Haweis in her book, *The Art of Beauty*, was writing adversely of this upholstered furniture: 'Every prop that should be straight and firm is bent and weakened—every curve of the body demanding accommodation reversed—and the whole outline is a miracle of lumpiness, vulgarity and unnaturalness.'

In later Victorian times easy chairs became less massive and solid. The area between the arms and the seat was often no longer filled with upholstery; the chair seats were lower and the whole structure lighter in appearance. Two such chairs can be seen either side of the fireplace in Fig. 109. An 'Art Furniture' example of the same type of chair can be seen in the left-hand foreground of Fig. 209. Two somewhat similar but simpler chairs upholstered in leather and made in the 1870s can be seen in Fig. 194. In the 1890s easy chairs took the outline which continued fashionable until the late 1930s and is still produced today. Such a chair can be seen at the fireside of the drawing room illustrated in Fig. 211.

Beside the large upholstered chairs with arms, there were innumerable smaller occasional chairs also upholstered. These were particularly popular in mid-Victorian drawing rooms and they were also used in bedrooms. Some examples are shown in Figs. 271–275.

Divans were particularly in favour from the early 19th century onwards. Before long this upholstered furniture began to invade the centre of the room, where it became a circular or rectangular upholstered seat called an ottoman (Fig. 279). Another Oriental form of furniture was the pouffe, a cylindrical upholstered seat with no woodwork visible. Seats called 'confidantes', 'tête-à-têtes' or 'sociables' were a further adaptation of this style of upholstered furniture, being a pair of seats joined on an S-plan in which two people could sit facing each other.

These pieces were elaborated and varied in many ways. There were confidantes for four persons all sitting rather as if on a merry-go-round; a confidante with an in-built table, no doubt for light refreshment, is shown in Figs. 280 and 281. A cross between a pouffe and a confidante for three people can be seen in the foreground of Fig. 109.

There were innumerable ways in which this type of furniture was made, and Richard Charles in his book of designs dated 1867 illustrates a piece (Fig. 63), which could divide into three separate parts; it is *en suite* with an armchair and upholstered single chair of more conventional design. Another example is illustrated in Fig. 282.

The divan and ottoman were names derived from the East. To many Victorians the East was legendary and wrapped in the picturesqueness imparted to it by the poets and painters; the Orient, indeed, possessed a curious fascination for the Western world. The wide reading of

Byron's poems in England, with their Near Eastern settings and their Albanian and Turkish characters, must have played a part in contributing to this interest in the East and its life, customs and manners.

In the *London Cabinet-Maker's Guide* (1873) there is a description of cheap Victorian upholstery which shows that its quality was on the same low level as the cheap cabinet ware:

'The stuffing of all the advertised "suites" is either hay or shavings; and for their "warranted suites, all hair and covered in satin, etc.," the horsehair is procured by the needy little trade-masters at the rag-and-bone shops, full of moth and filth, for about sixpence per pound, whilst the price of good curled hair, such as is used by honest tradesmen, costs from one-and-sixpence to two shillings per pound first hand from the manufacturers.'

Apart from making easy chairs and sofas, the upholsterers' trade was also kept busy in the supply of window curtains. During the first twenty-five years of the 19th century curtains were often highly elaborate in the design of their valances, but with the coming of the Victorian era they became more voluminous and trailed on the floor, with massive folds of materials to form the valances. Welby Pugin in *The True Principles of Pointed or Christian Architecture* (1841) makes some criticisms of the upholstery of this early Victorian period:

'Modern upholstery is made a surprising vehicle for bad and paltry taste, especially when anything very fine is attempted . . . enormous folds of stuff over poles, as if for the purpose of sale or of being dried, is quite contrary to the use and intentions of curtains, and abominable in taste; and the only object that these endless festoons and bunchy tassels can answer is to swell the bills and profits of the upholsterers, who are the inventors of these extravagant and ugly draperies, which are not only useless in protecting the chamber from cold, but are the depositories of thick layers of dust, and in London not unfrequently become the strongholds of vermin.'

The voluminous Victorian curtains went out in the second half of the period, when curtains became more restrained and followed the French style in the design of their valance.

The Victorian upholsterer also turned his attention to the chimney-piece, which previously had been left entirely alone by this tradesman. He fitted it with a mantel board, which was covered with material with a deep valance hanging from the front edge (Figs. 123, 142 and 227). This material was either the same as, or harmonised with, the other soft furnishings. The mantel board was no doubt popular with the householder who wished to save the expense of a new chimney-piece. Often existing 18th-century chimney-pieces were too narrow from back to front to take the typical Victorian marble clock and accompanying candelabra unless they were widened by the use of a mantel board; there was also the additional reason that many Victorians considered white marble chimney-pieces to be cold-looking and the more of them that was hidden the better.

It should be noted that in the 18th century the name was 'a chimney-piece' and the glass which hung over the chimney-piece was called 'a chimney glass.' In the Victorian period the name was 'a mantelpiece' and the looking glass above was termed 'an overmantel'.

The Victorian age merged imperceptibly, at the turn of the century, into the Edwardian age. There was no clean-cut dividing line. The work and influence of the individual designers of the late Victorian period, many of them associated in one way or another with the Arts and Crafts Movement, continued well into the reign of the Queen's son and beyond.

It has not been easy, because of its great span of time, in which so many changes in taste took place, to give a survey of the furniture of the reign of Queen Victoria; the photographic illustrations are there, however, for the reader to see for himself something of the various kinds of furniture the Victorians designed and lived with. That much of it was bad cannot be denied; all the same, if by examining the furniture they liked to have in their homes, we can add to our understanding of our Victorian ancestors, something will have been achieved.

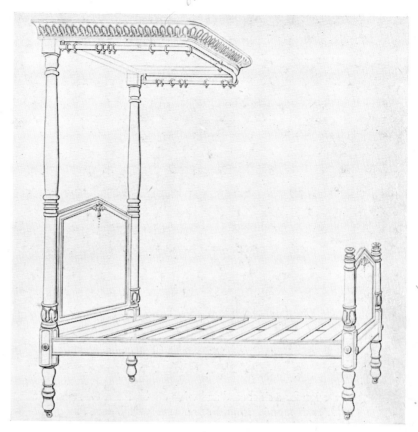

1. Half-tester bed from a trade catalogue *c.* 1840, issued by William Smee & Son, Finsbury Pavement, London. The illustration clearly shows how these beds were constructed. It is described in the catalogue as: 'A superior japanned canopy French bedstead with moulded cornice and a brass rod and rings.'

2. Design for a sideboard from Thomas Sheraton's *Cabinet Maker and Upholsterer's Drawing Book* (1792). The influence of the neo-classic style, still popular at the date of publication, can be seen in this piece.

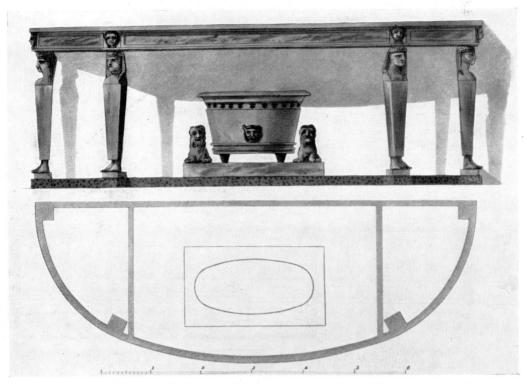

3. Design for a sideboard and wine cooler from George Smith's *A Collection of Designs for Household Furniture and Internal Decoration* (1808). By the date of publication the popularity of the neo-classic style had given place to a style which drew its inspiration from ancient Egypt.

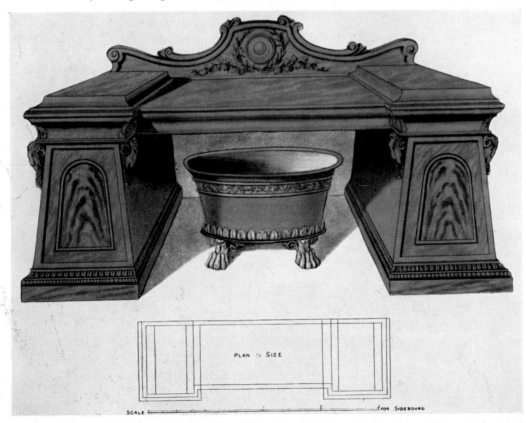

4. Design for a pedestal sideboard and wine cooler from George Smith's *Cabinet Maker and Upholsterer's Guide* (1826). Smith remarks in this book that his previous work, *Household Furniture*, had been rendered wholly obsolete by the rapid change and improvement in taste over the last twenty years. This design has the heaviness and solidity which is often associated with early Victorian furniture.

5. Design for a sideboard and cellaret from T. King's *The Modern Style of Cabinet Work* (1839). It is in a style often associated with late Regency furniture.

6. Interior illustrated in the *House Decorator and Painter's Guide*, produced in 1840 by a firm of decorators, H. W. & A. Arrowsmith. The authors described it as a 'perspective view of a design in the Elizabethan style suited for a Library'. A room such as this was considered an appropriate background for the 17th-century oak furniture then fashionable.

7. Illustration from the 1857 edition of J. C. Loudon's *Encyclopaedia of Cottage, Farm and Villa Architecture*. The author describes this drawing room as 'fitted up and furnished in the Gothic style'. The Victorians did not appreciate that it was Gothic in ornament only and that the structure on which Gothic details and motifs were applied was the same that was being used for furniture in other styles popular at the same date.

8. Illustration from the *House Decorator and Painter's Guide*. Skirting to cornice decoration in the rococo style of Louis XV was popular with the decorating and furnishing trades in the early Victorian period. When this style was used, the fireplace usually had a mirror over it and both the mirror frame and fireplace were decorated in harmony with the wall panels.

9. General view of part of the Furniture Court at the Great Exhibition in 1851. The Victorians saw nothing strange in the juxtaposition of the Louis XVth style table and chair on the left, the small Gothic style table nearby and the Elizabethan style bed in the middle distance. The piece on the left, incorporating the large mirror with the heavily carved frame at its back, would probably have been described as in the Italian style.

10. Design for a sideboard and wine cooler, made by Gillow of Lancaster and London, taken from *Furniture, Upholstery and House Decoration*. G. W. Yapp wrote of this piece: 'An example of the unconventional is refreshing now and then. Still, a new style cannot be evolved in a day, nor a year, nor perhaps in a dozen years, and the example before us can only be regarded as a praiseworthy attempt and an admirable specimen of wood-carving'.

12. Victorian sideboard formed of Elizabethan and Jacobean fragments of carving applied to a structure which had originally been a Jacobean court cupboard; in the reconstruction, the base of the court cupboard has been cut off.

11. Mid-Victorian oak armchair in the hall at Stradey Castle, Carmarthenshire. This folding chair is a close copy of a style current in the reign of Elizabeth I. (C. R. Mansel Lewis, Esq.)

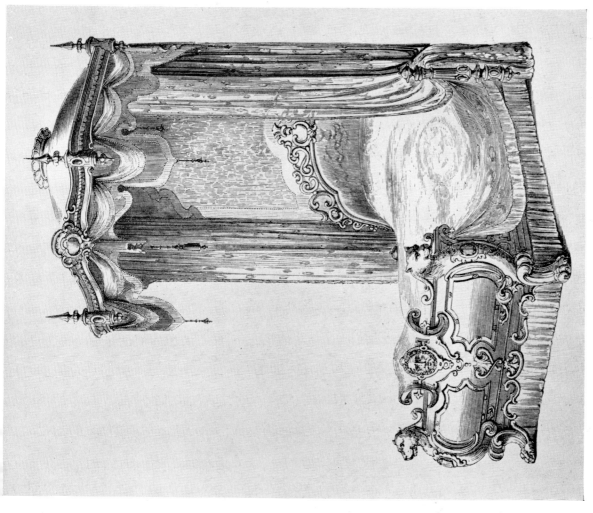

14. Design for a walnut half-tester bed by Thomas Fox, taken from *Furniture, Up-holstery and House Decoration*, edited by G. W. Yapp, an Assistant Commissioner and Compiler of the Official Catalogues of the Great Exhibition of 1851, writes: 'It is a State bed in the Elizabethan style, but judiciously treated in a lighter manner than is common.' This bed is also illustrated in Fig. 9.

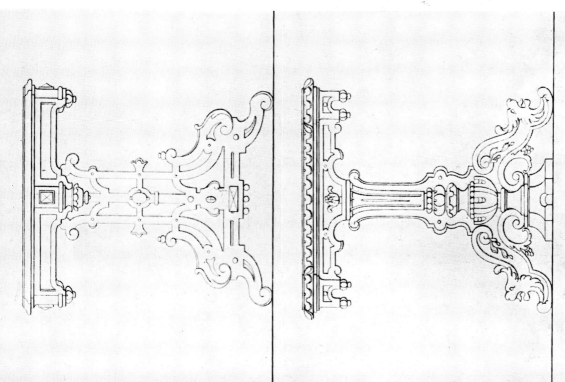

13. Illustration taken from Henry Whitaker's *House Furnishing, Decorating and Embellishing Assistant* (1847). These two designs for writing tables are described as 'Elizabethan' (top) and 'Renaissance' (bottom). Although Whitaker and his contemporaries thought he had designed each table in an entirely different style, it is realised today that the difference lay solely in the ornament.

15. Walnut and ebony carved cabinet by Freeman of Norwich. A writer in the *Art Journal Illustrated Catalogue* of the Great Exhibition of 1851 describes it as 'from a bold and well studied Italian design'. Today the mixed proportions of the design seem unfortunate. This example is fairly typical of the furniture sent to the Exhibition by provincial makers; in most cases they produced pieces of the greatest elaboration. 16. One pedestal and the backboard of the Charlecote Park sideboard (Fig. 17). The carving depicts scenes which the Victorians considered suitable for the dining room. The back panel shows boys tending the grape vines and the left pedestal shows corn being reaped. At either end of the backboard are clusters of dead game and fish realistically carved. (*The National Trust*)

17. Dining room at Charlecote Park, the seat of the Lucy family in Warwickshire. Mr and Mrs George Lucy redecorated their Elizabethan house in their generation's idea of that style. The dining room is hung with flock paper and furnished with a set of 'Elizabethan style' dining chairs and the firescreen, with a panel of Berlin woolwork, is of about the same date. The sideboard in the background is the work of J. M. Willcox of Warwick and his apprentice, Thomas Kendall; it was completed in 1858. (*The National Trust*)

18. The Kenilworth Sideboard or Buffet (Warwick Castle), made by Cookes of Warwick, is one of the best known pieces produced by the Warwickshire carvers. The back depicts the arrival of Queen Elizabeth at Kenilworth Castle; the left panel her meeting with Amy Robsart; and the right panel her interview with Lord Leicester. The upper part of the board is decorated with the coronet, arms and emblems of the Earls of Warwick. (*The Earl of Warwick*)

19. The back panel of the Kenilworth Sideboard (Fig. 18), depicting the arrival of Queen Elizabeth at Kenilworth Castle. (*The Earl of Warwick*)

21. Hinge and lock on one of the cupboard doors of the Alscot Park sideboard (Fig. 22). The lock plate incorporates the initials of the original purchaser. The piece has remained in the same house and in the possession of the same family.
(James Alston-Roberts-West, Esq.)

20. One of the large figures on the Kenilworth Sideboard or Buffet. There are four figures in all, one at each of the forward corners of the two pedestals; each depicts a prominent Elizabethan character. This one is Shakspeare. *(The Earl of Warwick)*

22. This sideboard at Alscot Park, Warwickshire, was made by Cookes of Warwick and shows a certain similarity to the Kenilworth sideboard. Unlike the example at Warwick Castle, however, it does not tell a particular story, but has a general theme of the chase. (*James Alston-Roberts-West, Esq.*)

23. Design for an Elizabethan style firescreen by Thomas H. Kendall for Mr Brooke Evans in 1861. (*D. W. Kendall, Esq.*)

24 and 25. Two table designs submitted by Thomas H. Kendall *c.* 1860 to Mr Douglas Evans. The two drawings are marked with Mr Evans's comments and initials, and the table that was eventually made for him incorporated the feet illustrated in Fig. 24 and the top illustrated in Fig. 25. (*D. W. Kendall, Esq.*)

26. Design for a looking glass in the Elizabethan style by Thomas H. Kendall, made for the Countess of Jersey c. 1860. (*D. W. Kendall, Esq.*)

27. Design for an 'Elizabethan' style chair by Thomas H. Kendall, drawn for Colonel L. V. Lloyd, c. 1860. (*D. W. Kendall, Esq.*)

28. Design for a looking glass and dressing table top by Thomas H. Kendall, prepared for Mr Douglas Evans in 1861. (*D. W. Kendall, Esq.*)

29. The Chevy Chase Sideboard, made between 1857 and 1863 by Gerrard Robinson of Newcastle. The six carved panels depict incidents recounted in the 'Ballad of Chevy Chase'. The sideboard is now at the Grosvenor Hotel, Shaftesbury. (*Trust Houses Ltd.*)

31. The top left hand panel of the Chevy Chase Sideboard depicts the arrival of Lord Douglas. The dead stags, which were poached by Hotspur and were the cause of the subsequent battle, lie in the foreground. (*Trust Houses Ltd.*)

30. Harry Hotspur was killed in the battle and the bottom right hand panel of the Chevy Chase Sideboard (Fig. 29) shows the return of his body to the castle of his father, the Earl of Northumberland. (*Trust Houses Ltd.*)

32. This copy of the *Bureau du Roi Louis XV* made by Pierre Dasson for the Marquess of Hertford in the mid–19th century is reputed to have cost 90,000 francs. The original bureau, at Versailles, was started in 1760 by J. F. Oeben and finished in 1769 by J. H. Riesener. (*Trustees of the Wallace Collection*)

33. Pedestal desk on which a rich, highly figured mahogany has been used for the veneer. The workmanship is of a high quality and the drawer linings are of oak. If not made in France, the piece is certainly made under French influence, which was very prevalent in English furniture in the 1860s. (*Anthony Coleridge, Esq.*)

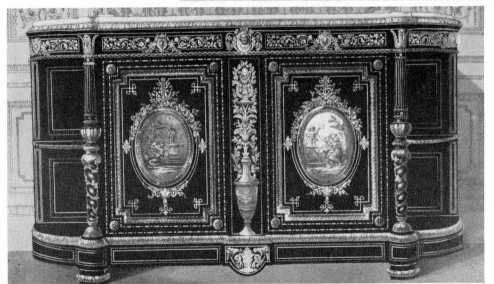

34. Cabinet by Jackson and Graham of London exhibited at the International Exhibition of 1862. J. B. Waring, in *Masterpieces of Industrial Art and Sculpture*, describes the piece as follows: 'It is made of ebony inlaid with ivory . . . with oval medallions of hymeneal subjects in bronze. . . . The style adopted is that of the best period of Louis Seize.'

35. Carved oak sideboard by Crace & Son exhibited at the International Exhibition of 1862. Although this piece was produced ten years after Pugin's death, J. B. Waring writes of it as follows: 'It bears the impression of Pugin's peculiar style; it was over 9 ft. in length and finely carved in oak in the style of the 15th century. The side panels were enriched with the vine, having scrolls each side; bearing the inscription "Wasshail" and "Trinkheile".'

36. Cabinet of carved and painted oak with wrought brass panels and fittings designed by Pugin. It is 8 ft. in height and was made by the firm of Crace & Son and exhibited in the Mediaeval Court at the Great Exhibition of 1851. (*Victoria and Albert Museum*)

37. Designs for four pieces of early Victorian furniture signed by Pugin and bearing the stamp of Crace & Son, of Wigmore Street. These designs do not indicate in any detail what the decoration is to be. Pugin appears to have been content to leave this to his friend, John G. Crace, whose descendants have retained this design among their papers.

38. Library table made by Crace & Son and probably inspired by rough sketches drawn by Pugin. The decoration is not, as might appear, painted but made from various inlaid woods. The table was made for Abney Hall, Cheshire, and remains in that house today. (*Cheadle & Gatley Urban District Council*)

39. Walnut cabinet book case with four glass doors and two wooden doors surmounted by a carved frieze. The door panels are decorated with marquetry carried out in many contrasting woods. This piece by Crace was probably based on a design by Pugin. Although only 4 ft. 6 ins. high, it can be compared with a piece in Fig. 36. (*Cheadle & Gatley Urban District Council*)

40. Cabinet in the Pompeian style exhibited at the International Exhibition of 1862 by J. H. Levien. Fourteen different woods were used, giving the cabinet a highly coloured appearance; they were, ebony, orange wood, purple wood, red sandal, amboyna, satinwood, pollard oak, hare-wood, sycamore, green maple, pear tree, walnut, holly (stained and natural), coco-nut wood. The two incised figures in the door panels are of ivory.

41. Book case, part of a suite by Howard & Sons, exhibited at the International Exhibition of 1862. G. W. Yapp describes the suite as follows: 'The aim of the artist was to reproduce the style and ornamentation of Herculaneum and Pompeii, and to adapt them to the requirements of our time.' 42. Carved ebony cabinet by H. Fourdinois, the younger, of Paris, exhibited at the International Exhibition of 1862. It was considered to be an exceptional work and was sold to an English collector for £1,400.

43. Cabinet of inlaid ebony made by Jackson and Graham from a design by R. S. Lorimer, exhibited at the International Exhibition of 1871. 44. Painted wardrobe by Dyer and Watts of London, exhibited in the Paris Exhibition of 1867. This piece made of pine had the decoration so neatly done in dark red colour that it gave the effect of inlaid wood. It was purchased by the Empress Eugenie of France.

45. Cabinet made by Wright and Mansfield, designed by Mr Crosse and exhibited at the Paris Exhibition of 1867, where it won the highest award. The cabinet is a fine example of the work of leading English firms in the 1860s; it is nearly 12 ft. high and made in satinwood, with elaborate marquetry of coloured woods, gilt mounts and mouldings and Wedgwood plaques. (*Victoria and Albert Museum*)

46. Mid-Victorian drawing room cabinet of thuya wood inlaid with contrasting black and white wood. It is decorated with three plaques and metal mounts. The two corner cupboards, with glass convex doors, would be for the display of objects probably either porcelain or silver. (*Mrs J. Pinto*)

47. Detail of the mounts, inlay and plaque of the mid-Victorian cabinet illustrated above. (*Mrs J. Pinto*)

48. Sideboard designed by W. J. Estall and made by James Lamb of Manchester. The piece is made of pollard oak, walnut and ebony with touches of gold. The two figures supporting the glass are life sized and executed in plain unpolished Italian walnut.

49. Sideboard designed by Robert Lorimer and made by Jackson and Graham. G. W. Yapp wrote: 'It is in the style of the Renaissance, executed in oak, the carved portions being left dead while the mouldings and framework are highly polished—an extremely effective arrangement.'

50 and 51. Dining room sideboard (*left*) and mantelpiece shelves (*right*) illustrated in *Hints on Household Taste*, by Charles L. Eastlake (1868). This style was known as 'Early English', its main feature being that the methods of construction were similar to those of mediaeval woodwork.

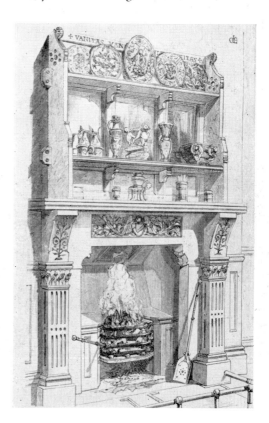

52 (*Above, left*). Wardrobe designed by Philip Webb. The door panels were painted by Edward Burne-Jones in 1858 with scenes from Chaucer's 'The Prioress's Tale'. This piece was a wedding present for William Morris, who himself painted the flowers on the side panels. It is now on permanent loan to the Victoria and Albert Museum. (*Ashmolean Museum, Oxford*)

53 (*Above*). Cabinet designed by Philip Webb and painted by Edward Burne-Jones in 1862. This piece is entitled 'The Backgammon Players' and although it shows Webb's simple methods of construction, the purpose of the piece is to provide a large, smooth surface for the artist to decorate; it should be judged more properly, therefore, by the quality of the painting rather than by the design of the structure. (*Metropolitan Museum of Art, New York*)

54. Hall chair of the early Victorian period made entirely of coal. The Victorians were always pleased if they could make furniture out of an unusual or unexpected material. (*John Rickett, Esq.*)

55. Oak table designed by Philip Webb, *c.* 1870. The massiveness of Webb's furniture can clearly be realised from this table and the one illustrated in Fig. 56. (*Victoria and Albert Museum*)

56. Circular table by Philip Webb, said to be the first piece of furniture he ever designed. It was almost certainly made by the inmates of the Euston Road Boys' Home about 1858. (*Dr D. C. Wren*)

57. Oak sideboard with carved boxwood panels and metal hinges, designed by Bruce Talbert. It was made by Gillow and exhibited in the London Exhibition of 1873.

58. Oak sideboard, carved and inlaid with contrasting woods, designed by Bruce Talbert. It was probably made in 1868, the year in which its original owner, Mr R. N. Thornton, commissioned nearly all the new furniture for his house at Sidmouth, Devonshire. It is very similar to a sideboard illustrated in Talbert's *Gothic Forms Applied to Furniture*, published the previous year (Fig. 60). (*Miss E. M. Thornton*)

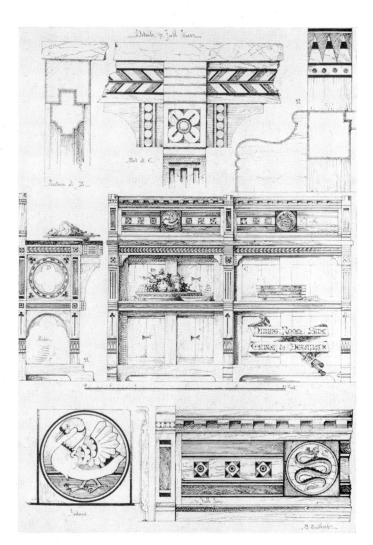

59 (*Above*). Side view of the sideboard illustrated in Fig. 58. It was probably made by Holland & Sons. This firm had the order to make most of the furniture for Mr R. N. Thornton's house and it is known that Bruce Talbert frequently designed for them. (*Miss E. M. Thornton*)

60 (*Above*). Design from Bruce Talbert's *Gothic Forms Applied to Furniture*, 1867. There are only slight differences between this and the sideboard in the possession of Miss E. M. Thornton, shown in Figs. 58 and 59.

61. Design for a Great Hall or dining room in Bruce Talbert's *Gothic Forms Applied to Furniture*. It shows that he did not consider his distinctive style should be confined to furniture alone, but applied to the entire decoration of a room.

62–66. Illustrations from a book of designs by Richard Charles. The oak sideboard, with the mirror back, is dated 1867. These pieces with their simple joined and plank construction are markedly similar to the work of his contemporaries, Eastlake and Talbert. Although Charles is less well known, his work is original and it was in the year of the dated plate, 1876, that Talbert produced his first book, which preceded by a year Eastlake's *Hints on Household Taste*.

67–70. Designs from a catalogue by G. M. & H. J. Story (1865). (*Above, left*) Card tables. (*Above, right*) Drawing room chairs and footstools. (*Left*) Chiffonier with centre door panel and back of mirror glass. (*Right*) Drawing room sofas.

71. Wash-stand at Castell Coch, Glamorgan, designed by John S. Chapple. The two unusual towers at each end contain water tanks. (*The Ministry of Works*)

72 (*Below, left*). Wash-stand designed by William Burges for his house in Melbury Road, London. (*Victoria and Albert Museum*)

73 (*Below, right*). Cabinet made in 1871 by Collinson and Locke, designed by T. E. Collcutt and made of ebonised mahogany with painted decoration. (*Victoria and Albert Museum*)

74. Mahogany sideboard designed by Christopher Dresser for Lord Hayter about 1880. The metal fittings are of brass and copper and the nine panels in the back are of beige stamped and gilt leather. (*Medical Missionary Association*)

75. Mahogany corner cupboard designed by Christopher Dresser for Lord Hayter about 1880. The metal fittings are of brass and copper and each door is set with a gilt metal plaque depicting a bird. (*Medical Missionary Association*)

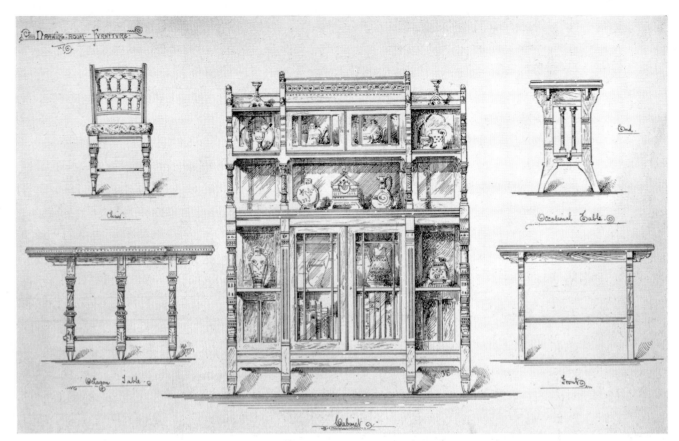

76. Designs for drawing room furniture in a catalogue entitled *Sketches for Artistic Furniture* (1872), by Collinson and Locke. The majority of the designs in this catalogue were by T. E. Collcutt.

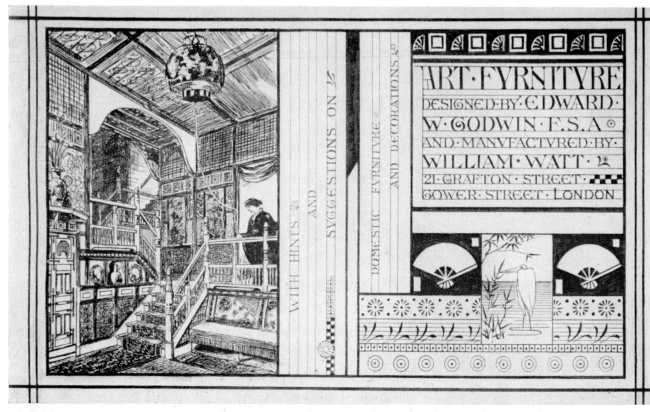

77. Title page from a catalogue entitled *Art Furniture*, published by Batsford in 1877. The designs were by E. W. Godwin and the furniture was made by William Watt. The decoration of this page clearly shows the influence of Japan on Godwin.

78. Sideboard of ebonised wood designed by Edward W. Godwin, influenced by oriental forms. It was made by William Watt about 1877. The metal fitments are silver plated and the inset panels are embossed leather. (*Victoria and Albert Museum*)

79. Coffee table and chair, both made of ebonised oak, designed by E. W. Godwin. The table was made in large numbers by William Watt and Collinson and Lock from about 1868. The chair, which has an upholstered seat and back, was made by William Watt about 1885. (*Victoria and Albert Museum*)

80. An 1880 design for some drawing room furniture by Jackson and Graham, illustrated by R. W. Edis in his *Decoration and Furniture of Town Houses*. The author says that this cabinet, made either in American walnut or mahogany, cost about £16; the little occasional table and the plain armchair with the split willow plaited seat cost about 30s. each.

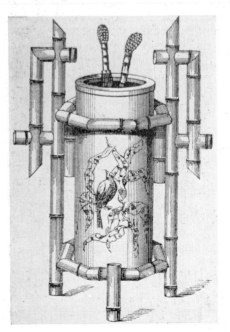

81. Design from the *Cabinet Maker and Art Furnisher*, illustrating a bamboo umbrella stand. 82. Desk made by Howard & Sons, of Berners Street, London, who have put their label inside two of the drawers. It is 3 ft. 8 ins. long; the superstructure is made of satinwood banded in contrasting wood and the legs are bamboo. (*C. Fredericks & Son*)

83. An 1880 design for three pieces of furniture by Holland & Sons, illustrated by R. W. Edis in his *Decoration and Furniture of Town Houses*. The author says that this group of furniture is made 'after old examples by Sheraton, Adam and Chippendale' and are 'good examples of the adaptation of the 18th-century designs to modern furniture'.

84. Design for a drawing room by Holland & Sons, *c.* 1885, in a style which they simply describe as '18th century'. Decorated or inlaid satinwood was more usual when this style was used, but here the furniture was of dark mahogany decorated by the firm's artists. (*Holland & Sons*)

86 (*Above*). Underside of the chair (*left*), showing the label of the maker, Howard & Sons, Ltd., of Berners Street, London. (*James A. Lewis and Son*)

85 (*Above*). Victorian mahogany armchair, with the splat decorated with Gothic tracery, in a style that was current *c.* 1755. This chair was made by Howard & Sons in the last quarter of the 19th century and has over the last eighty years acquired a good patination, which makes it hard to distinguish from an 18th-century example. (*James A. Lewis & Son*)

87. Cabinet of satinwood, with carved and painted decoration, made by E. Goodall & Co. *c.* 1886 and designed by A. H. Mackmurdo for the Century Guild. The inscription is a quotation from Shelley. This piece was exhibited in the Arts and Crafts Exhibition of 1888. (*William Morris Gallery, Walthamstow*)

88. Escritoire and stand made by Morris & Co. in 1893 and designed by George Jack. The floral marquetry is of sycamore and various other woods. (*Victoria and Albert Museum*)

89. Oak sideboard designed by W. R. Lethaby *c.* 1900. The piece is lightly carved and inlaid with ebony, sycamore and bleached mahogany. (*Victoria and Albert Museum*)

90 (*Above, left*). Oak cabinet, painted in red and gold, designed by C. R. Ashbee and made by the Guild of Handicraft in 1889. The piece is inscribed with quotations from William Blake's 'Auguries of Innocence'.
(*Abbotsholme School, Staffordshire*)

91 (*Above*). Oak desk with brass hinges designed by C. F. Voysey and made by W. H. Tingey in 1896. The heart was a favourite shape with Voysey, which he often used as ornament cut out on friezes and chair splats. This desk has no such ornamentation, although the hinges clearly show his liking for the heart.
(*Victoria and Albert Museum*)

92. Oak armchair and table, designed by Charles Rennie Mackintosh *c*. 1900. Almost all the furniture designed by Mackintosh is either in the possession of the Glasgow School of Art or the Glasgow City Corporation.
(*Glasgow School of Art*)

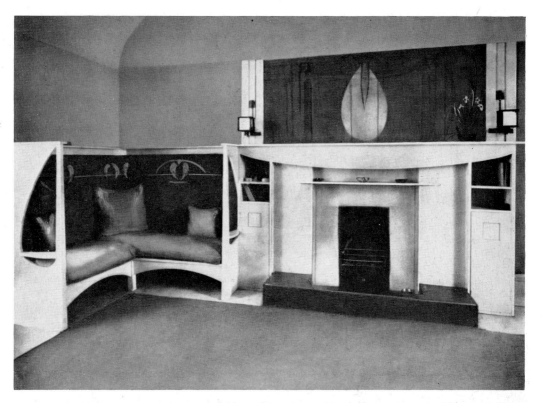

93. Drawing room fireplace and fitted corner seat at Dunglass Castle, East Lothian, designed by Mackintosh. He is the only Victorian furniture maker whose work has been fully catalogued; this was done by Thomas Howarth in his book, *Charles Rennie Mackintosh and the Modern Movement.*

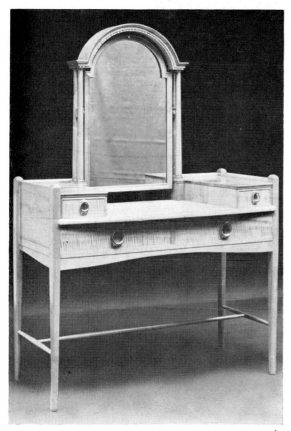

94. Toilet table in grey sycamore, with oxydised silver handles, designed by Ambrose Heal and made by his firm, Heal & Son, London. Only the early furniture of this designer was made before 1900. (*Heal & Son*)   95. Oak wardrobe inlaid with ebony and boxwood designed by Ambrose Heal and made by his firm. Heals, the Bath cabinet-makers and a few others continued in a more practical and commercial way to design in accordance with the best principles of the Arts and Crafts Movement. (*Heal & Son*)

96. Half-landing at 18, Stafford Terrace, London. The Victorians' love of plant life made conservatories very popular; in town houses, where space did not permit such a building, windows were often built out to form miniature green-houses. This example also includes a small aquarium. (*The Countess of Rosse*)

97. Stradey Castle, Carmarthenshire, is an entirely Victorian house. The main block with the three-gabled roof was built by the present owner's grand-father in 1840. The connecting wing and the tower were added in 1874. It did not seem incongruous to the Victorians to add on a heavily crenellated tower to a house which had no other signs of fortification; the tower, like the rest of the house, contains spacious bay windows in the lower part. (*C. R. Mansel Lewis, Esq.*)

98. Late 19th-century group of the Duke of Westminster's staff at Eaton Hall, Cheshire. It includes the organist of the private chapel and servants filling some now seldom heard-of posts. Among them are two grooms of the chambers, who were the senior upstairs men-servants, and a hall-boy responsible for carrying the staff food to the servants' hall and waiting in the housekeeper's room. Some of the men are in the uniform of the Duke's private fire brigade.

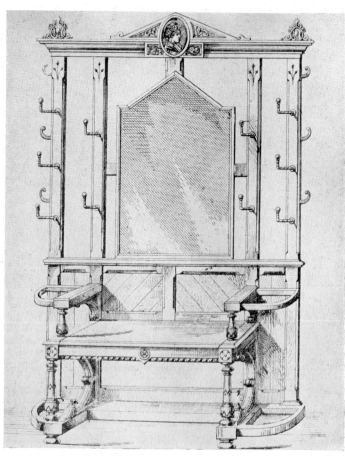

99. Design from a trade catalogue issued by William Smee about 1840. This hat and coat stand, combined with a rack and container for sticks and umbrellas, was intended to be placed against the wall.

100. Design for a hat, coat, stick and umbrella stand incorporating a mirror and a hall seat. This is illustrated in a trade catalogue issued by G. M. & H. J. Story, of London Wall, in 1865.

101. Design for a dining table by Thomas H. Kendall for Sir Charles Mordaunt, dated 1862. The table was 5 ft. 10 ins. wide and 7 ft. in length when closed. By the inclusion of additional leaves, it could be extended to 26 ft. The table had castors sunk into the feet to make it easier to extend. (*D. W. Kendall, Esq.*)

102 and 103. Oak bench (*above*) and table (*below*) in the Elizabethan style. These two pieces are part of a suite of hall furniture at Stradey Castle, Carmarthenshire. Hall furniture in the Elizabethan style was popular throughout the first half of the Victorian era. (*C. R. Mansel Lewis, Esq.*)

104. Dining room illustrated in a catalogue issued by Holland & Sons in the last quarter of the 19th century. This room, including the tapestry curtains and the Brussels carpet, could be furnished for about £100. In the middle class home the dining room was often also the second sitting room. (*Holland & Sons*)

105. Dining room in a medium sized house, photographed in the 1890s. The style is Elizabethan, which had been popular for halls and dining rooms from about 1840. The mantelpiece has also been given an Elizabethan appearance.

106. Mahogany pedestal sideboard with the centre enclosed by two doors and surmounted by a mirror in a carved mahogany frame. This piece was made about 1868 by Holland & Sons. (*Miss E. M. Thornton*)

107. Dining room at 18, Stafford Terrace. The wallpaper (by William Morris), the sideboard, the two chairs and the high shelf for the oriental porcelain are typical furniture and decoration for a person of taste and understanding in the 1870s. The oak sideboard, which shows the influence of C. L. Eastlake, is inset with panels depicting sprays of fruit painted in a Pre-Raphaelite style against a gold background. (See also Fig. 123.) (*The Countess of Rosse*)

144

108. Dining room at Stradey Castle, reproduced from a photographic plate taken about 1890. It remains virtually unchanged today. There are a large set of single dining chairs in the 'Elizabethan' style with a pair of carvers to match. (*C. R. Mansel Lewis, Esq.*)

109. Drawing room at Stradey Castle, also reproduced from an old photographic plate. The fireplace is of about 1840, but the upholstered furniture is of a later date; the draped material surround and the small shelves for porcelain round the over-mantel were no doubt added in the 1870s. (*C. R. Mansel Lewis, Esq.*)

110 and 111. Circular mahogany dining table *c.* 1835. It could be made to seat more people by the inclusion of eight slips of wood which increased the circumference. The table ready to receive these additional slips is shown below.
(A. B. C. Philips, Esq.)

113. Story's label on the balloon back chair (*left*). This firm's furniture was exported to many parts of the world. The chair on which this label appears is in Australia.

114 (*Below*). Underside of the chair, showing the position of the label. (*John Bonython, Esq.*)

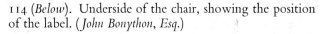

112. A mahogany balloon back chair with upholstered seat, made by G. M. & H. J. Story, of London Wall. After the first few years of the Victorian era, such chairs became universally popular and continued to be made until the end of the reign. (*John Bonython, Esq.*)

115. Two mid-Victorian balloon back chairs. The left hand one was intended for the drawing room and the right hand one for the dining room. Chairs with the balloon back were popular because of their comfort; this shape supported both the shoulders and the middle of the back. The back rails of the chair were curved for additional comfort. (*C. F. Wearn*)

116. Early Victorian dining room chair. This chair, apart from its turned front legs, retained much of the style of the Regency. This type of chair was quickly superseded by the balloon back chair.

117. Mid-Victorian walnut upholstered back chair with metal mounts. This chair, one of a set of eight, is an adaptation of the style of Louis XV. (*George J. Levy, Esq.*)

118. Design for two upholstered back chairs by Thomas H. Kendall, prepared for the Countess of Warwick about 1860. The deep buttoned back of the left-hand chair was a particularly popular style at this time. The price of the left-hand chair was four guineas and the right-hand one £4 10s. (*D. W. Kendall, Esq.*)

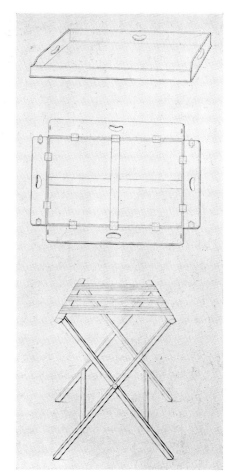

119 (*Left*). Designs for four dining chairs with upholstered backs from Story's catalogue, *c.* 1865. This style of chair succeeded the balloon back chair, although it did not by any means replace it, because the former style was cheaper to produce. Story's supplied middle class homes at medium prices.

120 (*Right*). Butler's tray illustrated in a trade catalogue of William Smee & Sons, Finsbury Pavement, *c.* 1840. It could either be used for carrying silver and glass, etc., or placed on its accompanying stand and used as an additional table.

121. Elegant mid-Victorian butler's tray. The table is made of rosewood and the two tiers, both of which have tray top edges, are an unusual feature. The total height is 2 ft. 9 ins. (*James A. Lewis & Son*)

122. Side table illustrated in the dining room section of Story's catalogue *c.* 1865. It was important in the dining room because it was used to place the dishes and plates on immediately before and after food was served.

123. Dining room at 18, Stafford Terrace, much as it was originally furnished in the 1870s. The pair of Victorian Windsor chairs are little changed in design from those of the 18th century. The centre light on pulleys, the mantelpiece shelves for the display of china, the fitted mantelboard covered with material and deep fringed valance are very typical of the date. (See also Fig. 107.) (*The Countess of Rosse*)

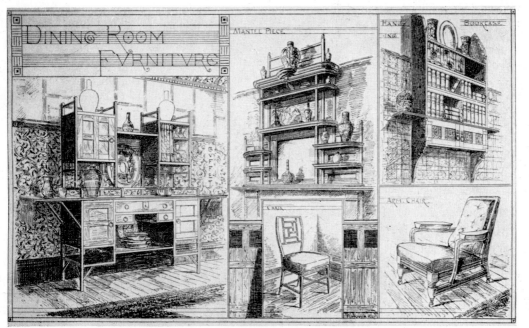

124. Design by E. W. Godwin from *Art Furniture*, a trade catalogue issued by William Watt in 1877. The cabinet is almost exactly the design for the piece illustrated in Fig. 78. Mantelpiece shelves were advocated by many leading designers and Godwin was no exception.

125. A mahogany chiffonier, *c.* 1840. Chiffoniers were originally intended for the morning room, but today they are often put to other uses. (*John Gloag, Esq.*)

126. A mahogany chiffonier, *c.* 1850. (*Mrs G. M. Gloag*)

127 and 128. Part of a morning room or drawing room suite, *c.* 1850. Above may be seen a pair of card tables and, below, a centre table. The centre table has an unusual two-tier carved edge (Fig. 130) and the same effect is given on the card tables by making the fixed leaf slightly larger than the folding one, so that they do not completely overlap. All three tables are mounted on castors. (*Restall, Brown & Clennell, Ltd.*)

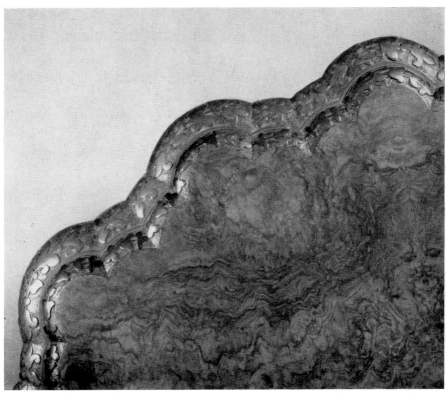

129–131. Part of the same suite shown in Figs. 127 and 128. Fig. 130 shows a detail of the edge of the centre table (Fig. 128). The other pieces are a pedestal jardinière and two of a set of chairs. The whole suite is made of walnut and where veneer is used, it is a brilliant figured burr-walnut.

132. Loo or circular table on a triangular pillar and base made of satinwood richly ornamented with ormolu and inlaid with contrasting woods. The table was made by Holland & Sons and their records state that it was 'old stock' and supplied to Mr R. N. Thornton in 1868 for £38 18s. (*Miss E. M. Thornton*)

133. Triangular base and pillar of the circular table (*above*), showing the elaborate ormolu mounts. This table may have been intended for the music room of Mr Thornton's house. (*Miss E. M. Thornton*)

134 and 135. Davenport in walnut shown both closed and open. This piece of furniture was popular throughout the early and middle Victorian periods. The drawers were nearly always down the side. In this example the top folds back and a slide pulls forward to make a miniature desk; at the same time part of the top springs up to reveal three drawers and four pigeon holes. The construction is quite different from the sloping top shown in the davenport below. (*S. A. Pollitt, Esq.*)

136-139. Davenport in satinwood with banding and lines of rosewood made by Gillow & Sons in the early Victorian period. It is in the style of a school desk, the flat, sloping top being intended for writing on. On the right are the maker's name stamp, a drawer front and the bottom of a drawer, showing a typical Victorian construction, in which the drawer bottom was let into a grooved drawer slip, either pinned or glued to the drawer side. (*James A. Lewis & Son*)

141. Walnut writing cabinet made by Holland & Sons and almost identical to the example on the left. It, however, is not so richly decorated and whereas the other has metal mounts and an elaborate escutcheon and key, this is edged with contrasting wood and has a plain lock. (*James A. Lewis & Son*)

140. Walnut writing cabinet with cupboard below, made by Holland & Sons c. 1868. The top falls forward to provide the writing surface and the upper part is fitted with drawers and pigeon holes. In this respect it is similar in design to the writing cabinets made about 1700. (*Miss E. M. Thornton*)

156

142. Morning room at 18, Stafford Terrace much as it was originally decorated and furnished in 1874. As in the dining room (Fig. 123) and drawing room (Frontispiece) there is a high rail for the display of oriental china; the mantelpiece shelves are, however, more elaborate than those in the dining room. The pair of inlaid satinwood china cabinets on either side of the fireplace are a Victorian version of the style that had been made popular a hundred years earlier by the Adam brothers. (*The Countess of Rosse*)

143. Morning room at 18, Stafford Terrace. The arrangement of plates, pictures, Japanese prints, needlework pictures, drawings and water colours and the Hepplewhite style suite, of which the sofa and one chair can be seen, shows the catholic taste of Linley Sambourne, who originally furnished the house. (*The Countess of Rosse*)

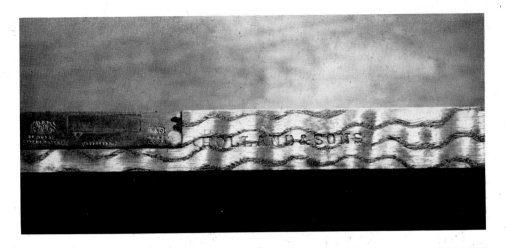

144. The name stamp of Holland & Sons, which is to be found on much of the furniture they supplied. By mid-Victorian times the practice of stamping drawer edges or tops of cupboard doors was usual with the leading furniture makers. (*Miss E. M. Thornton*)

145. Loo table and card table 'en suite' taken from an early Victorian catalogue of about 1840.

146. Early Victorian rosewood loo table; the design is still influenced by the style of the Regency. (*Mrs Hammond*)

147 and 148. Early Victorian loo tables. On the left is a mahogany veneered table, with a white marble top and moulded border. On the right is a rosewood example, with a glass top. (*C. Silburn & Sons*)

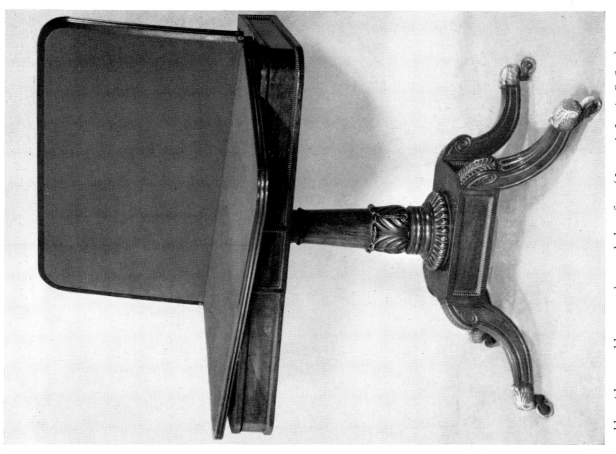

149 and 150. Two early Victorian rosewood tables. On the left is a circular table with a marble top and carved claw feet. (*James A. Lewis & Sons*) On the right is a card table which still shows the influence of the Regency. (*C. F. Wearn*)

151. Early Victorian rosewood occasional table retaining some of the decoration of the Grecian style of the Regency. (*C. Silburn & Sons*)

152. Early Victorian circular table made of burr elm with carved legs and stretcher of unusual design. (*James A. Lewis & Son*)

153 and 154. (*Left*) Occasional table, *c.* 1850, of walnut with an inlaid top. (*C. Silburn & Sons*) (*Right*) Small high circular table on tripod base, of walnut with an elaborately inlaid top of strapwork design entwined with foliage in various woods on a background of dyed sycamore. (*George J. Levy, Esq.*)

155. (*Left*) Small circular occasional table on carved tripod feet, made about 1850. (*Right*) Early Victorian work table on a triangular base, made about 1840. (*R. W. Paul, Ltd.*)

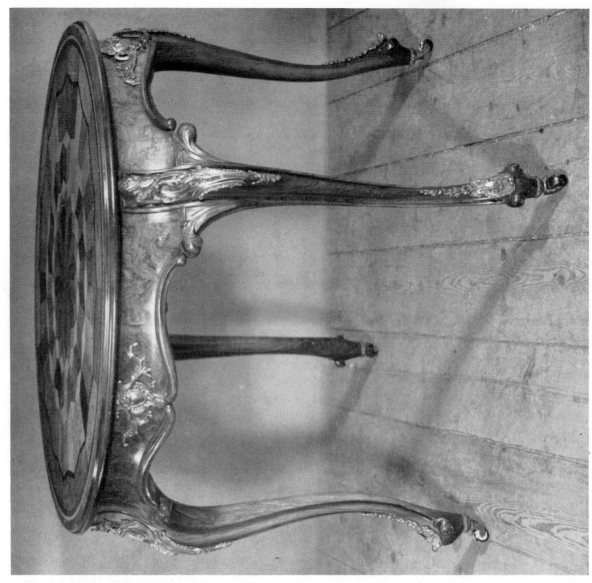

156 and 157. Types of Victorian table. (*Left*) A mid-Victorian walnut occasional table. (*George J. Levy, Esq.*) (*Right*) Circular occasional table *c.* 1850, with legs of solid walnut and frieze veneered with burr-walnut. There are ormolu mounts and the top is decorated with a geometric design in contrasting woods. (*H. Blairman & Sons, Ltd.*)

158 and 159. Examples of occasional table. (*Left*) An occasional table of high quality, with a parquetry inlaid top and a quadruped carved and inlaid base. (*Philip Blairman, Esq.*) (*Right*) Design for a small circular occasional table drawn by Thomas H. Kendall in 1864. (*D. W. Kendall, Esq.*)

160. Mid-Victorian tea table of amboyna wood with a shaped top and zebra wood cross bandings. The cluster column legs and the fretwork brackets, that give the table a Gothic appearance, are reminiscent of 18th-century design. (*James A. Lewis & Son*)

161. Pair of mid-Victorian card tables each supported by four columns on moulded legs with incised decoration. (*C. Silburn & Sons*)

162. Design for a table drawn by
Thomas H. Kendall in 1864.
(*D. W. Kendall, Esq.*)

163. Circular or loo table with
quadruped base moulded and
decorated with brass mounts; the
piece, made about 1860, has a top
of figured walnut veneer.
(*Philip Blairman, Esq.*)

164. Circular or loo table made about 1860 and supported on five columns and four feet, ornamented with incised decoration. The top is inlaid. (*C. F. Wearn*)

165. Circular table of amboyna wood decorated and edged in contrasting woods and enriched with ormolu mounts. This piece, with its elegantly designed feet and four supporting pillars, could only have been made by a leading firm of cabinet makers. (*H. Blairman & Sons, Ltd.*)

166. Thuya wood circular table supported by four pillars and feet, all richly ornamented with ormolu mounts. This very fine piece was made by Holland & Sons in 1868 for Mr R. N. Thornton. (*Miss E. M. Thornton*)

167 and 168. (*Right*) Detail of the pillars, feet and mounts of the table shown above. (*Below*) Inlay on the top of the same table. The inlaid circle of lilies of the valley, which continues round the entire border of the table, shows extremely well against the veneered thuya wood surface of the table. (*Miss E. M. Thornton*)

170. Rosewood table on four carved feet made about 1850; the top is decorated with an inlaid draughts or chess board and the drawer is elaborately fitted with necessities for sewing. (*George J. Levy, Esq.*)

169. Work table made about 1840 of walnut and part veneered with curiously figured mahogany. The top is inlaid with fiddleback satinwood and mahogany. (*George J. Levy, Esq.*)

171. Mid-Victorian walnut occasional table with a rack below to contain books. Innovations were typical of the Victorian period, but they were not always as practical and useful as this one. (*George J. Levy, Esq.*) 172. Octagonal occasional table supported by four turned carved pillars and stretcher with four shaped legs on castors. (*Miss E. M. Thornton*)

173. Mid-Victorian
burr-elm and
burr-ash work
table; the
gadrooned edge and
turned and carved
stretcher are of oak.
(*George J. Levy, Esq.*)

174. Mid-Victorian
walnut table with
circular top and
two drop leaves.
These tables, with a
cloth placed on
them, were used for
afternoon tea. They
were usually fitted
with castors so that
they could be
moved easily to the
required position.
(*Philip Blairman, Esq.*)

175. Mahogany table with two drop leaves and a shaped top. The legs, feet and stretcher are of unusual design. (*Mrs Hammond*)

176. The table shown above in the closed position. It is at present at Benacre Hall, Suffolk. (*Mrs Hammond*)

173

177 and 178. Satin-wood table made in 1868 by Holland & Sons. It is in the style of Louis XV and is richly ornamented with marquetry and decorated with ormolu mounts. (*Below*) Shaped top of the table shown above, showing the elaborate floral marquetry with a centre panel of musical instruments. The musical instruments are incorporated in many of the pieces of furniture made for Mr R. N. Thornton's house, Knowle Cottage, Sidmouth. (*Miss E. M. Thornton*)

179. Designs for six drawing room chair backs taken from T. King's *Cabinet Work Supplement* (1840). A suggestion of the balloon back, which was later to become universally popular, can be seen in two of these designs.

180. Designs for three early Victorian parlour chairs; the right-hand chair is an early example of the balloon back style which continued to be made throughout the Victorian period.

181. Early Victorian balloon back chair made by Gardner & Son, of Aldgate, London. Similar chairs can be seen in the painting of a drawing room (Fig. 207). (*John Bonython, Esq.*)

182. An adaptation of a balloon back chair which contains an upholstered panel in the back. The walnut chair, *c.* 1860, is one of a set of six. (*George J. Levy, Esq.*)

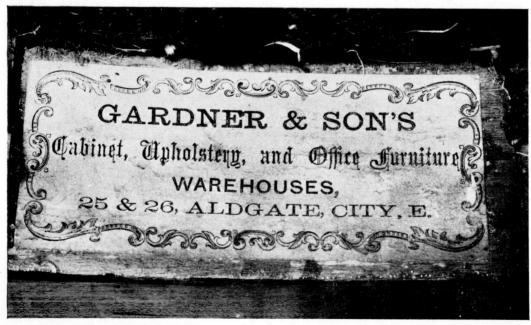

183. The label of Gardner & Son pasted on the rail of the chair shown above (*left*).

184. Mid-Victorian walnut chair, possibly one of a set intended for a dining room. (C. F. Wearn)

185. Chair with upholstered seat and back panel, made of walnut. This style was frequently described by Victorians as 'Eliza-bethan', although it more closely resembles that of the Restoration period. (C. F. Wearn)

186. Rosewood chair, inspired by the Caroline cane chair, and a table on twisted pillars and tripod feet which has a view of Windsor Castle painted on the top. Both these pieces are mid-Victorian. (C. Silburn & Sons)

187. Chair designs drawn in 1862 by Thomas H. Kendall for Sir Charles Mordaunt. Both chairs show alternative designs for the front legs and back. (*D. W. Kendall, Esq.*)

188. One of a pair of rosewood foot stools with needlework tops made about 1865. The box key pattern is in rosewood inlaid with sycamore. (*George J. Levy, Esq.*)   189. A good example of a mid-Victorian walnut stool. (*Philip Blairman, Esq.*)

190. Oval backed arm chair made in the 1860s, copying the style popular in late 18th-century France. The chair, which is of high quality, is made of padouk with purplewood cross bandings and enriched with metal mounts; it was certainly made by a leading maker. (*Philip Blairman, Esq.*)

191. Oval backed rosewood armchair. This piece is similar in style to the chair (Fig. 190), but was probably made a few years earlier; it has an altogether heavier appearance and would have been made by the general furniture trade rather than by a leading cabinet-maker. (*Mrs Hammond*)

192. Chair (*left*) with the seat rail and back made in a continuous curve. This style of chair is very comfortable and could be considered the forerunner of the modern deck chair. Stool (*right*) with needlework top and turned stretcher on heavily carved legs, made about 1850. (*C. Silburn & Sons*)

193. Mid-Victorian chair made in oak, at Stradey Castle, Carmarthenshire. The arrangement of the legs is an adaptation of the style used for mid-18th-century writing chairs. (*C. R. Mansel Lewis, Esq.*)

194. Bay window of the dining room at 18, Stafford Terrace, London, showing two oak chairs upholstered in leather and an oak cupboard all made about 1870. The simple construction of the stretchers on the right hand chair shows the influence of the Arts and Crafts Movement. The enclosed window box in the centre window is an example of the Victorians' love of plant life. (*The Countess of Rosse*)

195 and 196. (*Left*) Mid-Victorian what-not veneered in walnut and inlaid with tulipwood. The fluted columns are picked out in gold and the feet are mounted on castors; a brass gallery surrounds three sides of the top.
(*Right*) Mid-Victorian what-not of thuya wood with walnut crossbanding. These pieces of furniture were used for the display of ornaments, china, porcelain and silver and also for books and papers. There are records of such pieces as early as 1800.
(*George J. Levy, Esq.*)

197. Mid-Victorian secretaire entirely veneered in tulipwood. The contrasting effects are achieved by placing the veneer so that the grain runs in different directions. The inside of the secretaire drawer is veneered in rosewood and the drawer linings are of finest oak. A piece of this quality would have been made only by one of the leading makers and its cost would have been considerable. (*George J. Levy, Esq.*)

198. Detail of the door panel and ormolu mounts on the secretaire (Fig. 197).

199. Mid-Victorian two-tier walnut cabinet with ormolu mounts, intended either for the display of objects or as a glass fronted book case. (*C. Silburn & Sons*) 200. Mid-Victorian cabinet of thuya wood inlaid with contrasting woods and decorated with ormolu mounts, with an oval mirror in the centre panel. This piece is at Benacre Hall, Suffolk. (*Mrs Hammond*)

201 and 202. Firescreens were almost universal in Victorian reception rooms in the first half of the period; sometimes they were on two pairs of feet joined by a stretcher and sometimes on a tripod with the screen attached to a single pole. The making of bead and needlework panels for these screens was a popular pastime with Victorian ladies. (*Left*) Firescreen with needlework panel made about 1850. (*Mrs Hammond*) (*Right*) The crossbar of this mid-Victorian example, holding the shield-shaped panel of embroidery, can be moved up and down the centre pole to the required height. (*Philip Blairman, Esq.*)

185

203. Very fine drawing room cabinet made by Holland & Sons in 1868, of satinwood heavily enriched with ormolu, with many additional woods used for the banding and inlay, including boxwood, rosewood, hare-wood and walnut; ivory is also used. The original cost of the cabinet was £77 10s.

(*Miss E. M. Thornton*)

205. Cabinet with shaped open ends and corner shelves backed by mirror glass, supplied by Holland & Sons in 1868; it is made of satinwood inlaid with many contrasting woods and richly mounted with ormolu. (*Miss E. M. Thornton*)

204. Satinwood corner cupboard similar in design to the cabinet shown in Fig. 203. A pair of these cupboards, made by Holland & Sons in 1868, cost £45. (*Miss E. M. Thornton*)

206. Large cabinet with display shelves backed with mirror glass and with two cupboards enclosed by doors with marquetry panels. The piece, like Figs. 203, 204 and 205, is made of satinwood with ormolu mounts and inlaid with contrasting woods.
(*Miss E. M. Thornton*)

207. A painting of an early Victorian drawing room with typical furniture of the period. The set of chairs are balloon backed and the circular table is supported on a tripod base. The chandelier contains three colza oil lamps. There are no doubt double doors folded back out of sight, which could be closed to divide the room into two separate apartments.

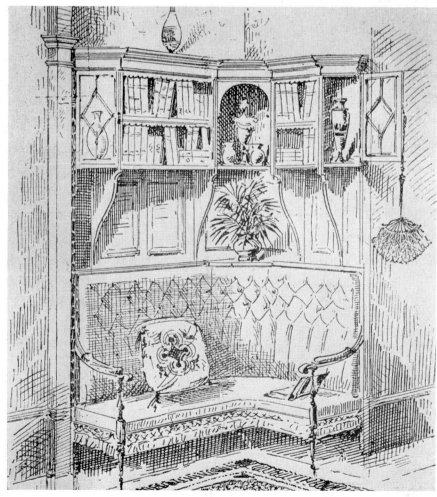

208. Cosy corner illustrated by E. Knight in his pamphlet, *Taste and Economy in Decoration and Furniture* (1893). Cosy corners were a popular feature in many late Victorian homes and survived even into the 20th century. The shelves held books and ornaments of all kinds.

209. Drawing room illustrated in William Watt's trade catalogue, entitled *Art Furniture* (1877). The design is by E. W. Godwin and the style was considered to be Japanese. The cabinet partly shown in the left-hand corner is typical of Godwin's style. The wallpaper is oriental in design and the picture frieze may well have been imported from Japan.

210. The 'Great Parlour' of Wightwick Manor, Wolverhampton, built in 1895 to the designs of Edward Ould. This contemporary photograph shows the panels of William Morris's 'Diagonal Trail' on blue serge and a wing chair up-holstered in Morris material. The varied origin of the objects in the room is typical of late Victorian taste.

(*Sir Geoffrey Mander*)

211. Drawing room illustrated in E.
Knight's *Taste and Economy in Decoration
and Furniture* (1893). This room still has a
rail for the display of porcelain, although
the mantelpiece shelves have disappeared.
Styles here are very mixed; the glass
fronted china cabinet, with two drawers
below, suggests the influence of English
furniture of the mid-18th century; the
occasional table in the centre is vaguely
reminiscent of the style of Louis XV; the
settee, the white chair and the desk chair
show the influence of the Arts and Crafts
Movement and mix unhappily with the
elaborate rococo screen by the fire. The
surround to the fireplace, with its pillars
and pediment, is an unfortunate
combination with the lattice cottage type
windows.

212. Design for a heavily carved book
case by Thomas H. Kendall, which has
what the Victorians considered to be
Elizabethan decoration; it includes in the
upper frieze the bear and ragged staff,
the crest of the Earl of Warwick, for
whom the piece was intended.
(*D. W. Kendall, Esq.*)

213. Dwarf break-front book case of walnut with ebonised columns and mouldings, made during the first half of the 19th century. The wings have ormolu grilles and the centre part glazed doors. The friezes of the two wings are fitted with drawers. (*James A. Lewis & Son*)

214. Part of the top of the dwarf book case seen above. The top is covered with leather with a tooled edge, surrounded by a border made of various inlaid woods. (*James A. Lewis & Son*)

215. Mahogany break-front book case decorated by eight columns; the mouldings are carved and the whole piece is of highly figured mahogany. Book cases of this style were popular in the first half of the Victorian period and a very simliar piece is illustrated in J. C. Loudon's *Encyclopaedia*. (*Bayliss, Jones & Bayliss, Ltd.*)

216. The library at Sheringham Hall, Norfolk. The house was built between 1812 and 1817, but the book cases were not made until 1839. This is a compromise between the completely fitted book cases in libraries of the late 18th century and the large free-standing book cases popular in Victorian times (an example of which is shown in Fig. 215). (*Thomas Upcher, Esq.*)

217. Dwarf book case with turned and carved columns made of walnut and of a design popular in the early Victorian period. (*John Gloag, Esq.*)

218. Cabinet book case of satinwood inlaid with purplewood, supplied by Holland & Sons to Mr Thornton in 1868 for £57 10s. This book case was probably intended for the drawing room or boudoir, unlike the other examples illustrated in previous pages, which were for the study or library. (*Miss E. M. Thornton*)

219. Large mahogany pedestal desk made by Wright and Mansfield of Bond Street. This firm were one of the leading producers of high quality furniture and specialised in the styles of Adam and Chippendale.

220. Edge of the centre drawer of the pedestal desk (*above*), showing the lock and the maker's name stamped in the wood.

221. Desk supplied by Holland & Sons to Mr Thornton in 1868. Holland's accounts describe the piece as 'A walnut and tulipwood kidney shaped writing table mounted with a brass gallery—£27 10s. 0d.' (*Miss E. M. Thornton*)

222. Satinwood escritoire in Louis XV style made by Holland & Sons. The piece is very light and elegant and inlaid with trellis and bands of fancy woods; it is enriched with ormolu mounts and the inside is lined with velvet. (*Miss E. M. Thornton*)

223. The central mount of the escritoire (*above*). The date shown—1868—is the year of manufacture. Holland's records show that it was originally supplied for the boudoir at a cost of £64 10s. (*Miss E. M. Thornton*)

197

224. Mid-Victorian kidney-shaped writing table made of burr-walnut. This piece, with its elegant legs and stretcher, gives an altogether lighter effect than the similarly shaped piece in Fig. 221. (*George J. Levy, Esq.*)

225. Unusual shaped pedestal desk of thuya wood with a covered leather top; the drawers are banded in contrasting wood and mahogany lined. This mid-Victorian desk was made by Gillow of Lancaster, who stamped their name on the edge of the centre top drawer. (*Leonard Knight, Ltd.*)

226. Bedroom illustrated in a catalogue published by Holland & Sons in the last quarter of the 19th century. The furniture illustrated in this room (excluding the bed) was supplied in three woods at different prices— polished pine: £22, polished ash: £30, walnut: £36. Besides the furniture shown in the illustration, the price included two additional cane seated chairs, a pedestal cupboard and a towel rail. (*Holland & Sons*)

227. Double bedroom illustrated in E. Knight's *Taste and Economy in Decoration and Furniture*. It cannot be seen from the illustration whether the bed is a half-tester, although this is unlikely to be the case in 1892 when Cooper and Holt produced the illustration. The mantelpiece board includes curtains; the two wardrobes and the overmantel have been treated as one and are a precursor of 20th-century fitted bedroom furniture. This bedroom, with its chaise-longue and sensible furniture, is altogether more satisfactory than the drawing room by the same firm (Fig. 211).

229. Large early Victorian mahogany dressing table mirror, at Stradey Castle, Carmarthenshire. (*C. R. Mansel Lewis, Esq.*)

228. Half-tester bed with provision for side curtains only, illustrated in *Designs for Furniture*, by John Dwyer (1857). This bed, with its simple lines and lack of decoration, is surprisingly plain by mid-Victorian standards.

230. Fine quality pedestal dressing table made in the late 1860s by Holland & Sons, who charged £34 15s. for it. The piece is made of Hungarian ash with mouldings and inlaid lines of purplewood. (See also Fig. 234.) (*Miss E. M. Thornton.*) 231. Wardrobe with the centre panel of looking glass. This piece, ebonised and decorated in gold, was part of a suite made by Heal & Son in the late 19th century for the State Bedroom at Ragley Hall, Warwickshire. (*Marquess of Hertford*)

232. Large pedestal dressing table of satinwood inlaid with kingwood, made by Wright and Mansfield. The bedroom suite includes a commode seat, towel rail and wardrobe, the latter being illustrated below. The pieces are of a very fine quality and cedar lined. (*Quinneys Ltd., Chester*)

233. Large break-front wardrobe of satinwood inlaid with kingwood. Wright and Mansfield, of Bond Street, London, made this piece, which is cedar lined and part of a double bedroom suite. (*Quinneys Ltd., Chester*)

234. Hungarian ash wardrobe with mouldings and inlaid lines of purplewood supplied by Holland & Sons in the late 1860s. It cost the then not inconsiderable sum of £68 10s. (See also Fig. 230.) (*Miss E. M. Thornton*)

235. Pedestal of drawers of Hungarian ash inlaid with purplewood, the top edged by a brass gallery, supplied by Holland & Sons in 1868 at a cost of £16 10s. (*Miss E. M. Thornton*)

236. Design for a console table surmounted by a looking glass with a frame carved to match, in *Designs for Furniture*, by John Dwyer (1857).

237. Design for a smoking room in the Turkish style, from a catalogue issued by Holland & Sons towards the end of the 19th century. (*Holland & Sons*)

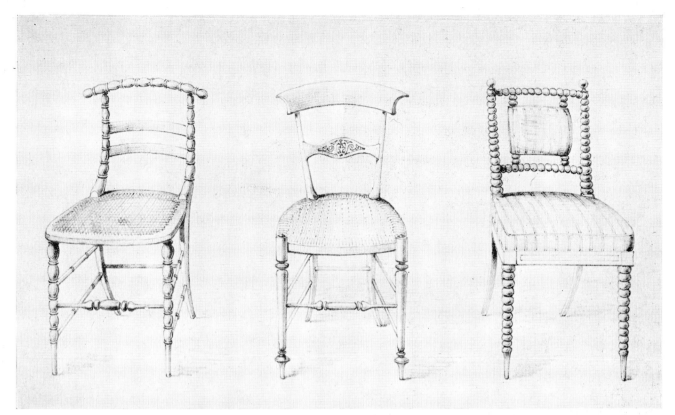

238. Designs for three bedroom chairs from an early Victorian trade catalogue. The centre chair, apart from the rush seat, is of a style that could have been used in the drawing room.

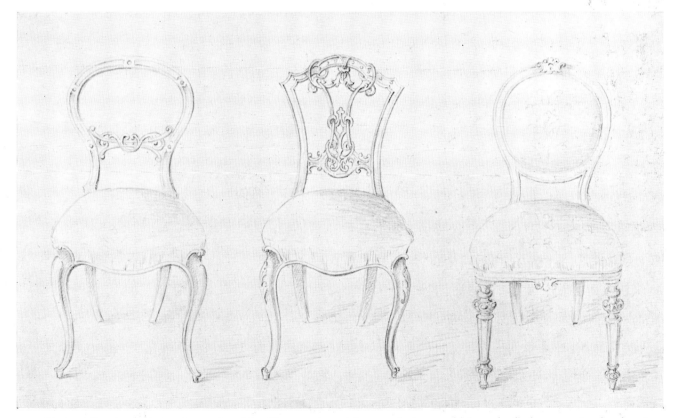

239. Designs for three chairs drawn in 1861. These rather elaborate chairs would have looked correct in the drawing room and it is only that their designer, Thomas H. Kendall, has written on 'Design for bedroom chairs' that we know for what they were intended. (*D. W. Kendall, Esq.*)

240 and 241. (*Left*) Door panel of the cabinet illustrated in Fig. 206, showing the fine marquetry design of flowers, ribbons and musical instruments carried out in many woods. This work is of the highest quality. (*Right*) Centre door panel of the cabinet illustrated in Fig. 203. The design of a medallion with an urn in the centre, surrounded by swags, flowers and ribbons, is beautifully executed in many contrasting woods. Both this and the marquetry panel (*left*) are the work of Holland & Sons in 1868. (*Miss E. M. Thornton*)

242. Mid-Victorian
Buhl china cabinet.
Buhl-work was
particularly popular
for china cabinets
and commodes,
although other pieces
of furniture,
particularly small
tables, were
decorated.
It was complicated
work and even
in cheaper examples,
when turtleshell was
used instead of
tortoiseshell,
considerable care had
to be exercised by
the craftsmen.
(*Green & Hatfield*)

207

243. Door panel of the Buhl cabinet (Fig. 242). In this piece the brass parts are plain, but with high quality Buhl work these portions of the design were carefully engraved, giving the piece an additionally light and attractive appearance. (*Green & Hatfield*)

244. Detail of the corner cupboard (Fig. 204), showing the frieze decorated with elaborate ormolu mounts and the corner mount in the form of a ram's head with swags. The small screws fixing the mounts can be seen. (*Miss E. M. Thornton*)

245. Detail of the mounts of the cabinet with shaped open ends (Fig. 205). The elaborateness of this piece can be realised from the decoration in inlaid wood and ormolu. The whole effect is light and elegant. (*Miss E. M. Thornton*)

246. Model of T. B. Jordan's woodcarving machine. The machine, invented in 1845, would appear to have been the first completely successful machine of its type. (*Science Museum, South Kensington*)

247 (*Below, left*). Lobby chair illustrated in J. C. Loudon's *Encyclopaedia of Cottage, Farm and Villa Architecture and Furniture*. He writes that the design is 'Etruscan' and drawn by Mr Mallet.

248 (*Below*). Design for an iron elbow kitchen chair from Loudon's *Encyclopaedia*. He writes: 'The back and elbow are cast in one piece; the supports for the elbows and also the legs are of gas tubing, screwed into a cross frame of iron, which proceeds from the back of the chair under the wooden seat.'

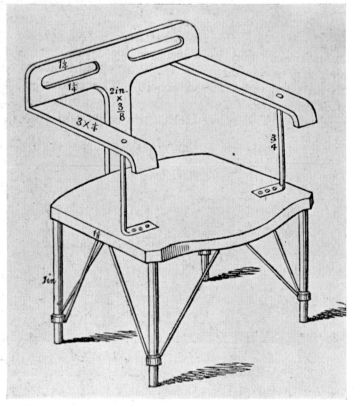

249. Mid-Victorian papier mâché chiffonier, illustrated in *Furniture, Upholstery and House Decoration*, edited by G. W. Yapp. This piece was made by Jennens and Bettridge, who were the leading manufacturers of high quality papier mâché in the Victorian period.

250. Elegant and unusual papier mâché piece, incorporating two mirrors, decorated with a painted design and inlaid with mother of pearl. The bird and the butterfly, on either side of the upper mirror, are cleverly portrayed in mother of pearl and are again repeated on the top. (*Mrs Hughes*)

251. Papier mâché half-tester bed. The structure is made of iron and only the applied decoration, the headboard and footboard are of papier mâché. (*Victoria and Albert Museum*)

212

252. Light and elegant papier mâché chair on castors with a cane seat; there is gold painted decoration and an inlay of mother of pearl. The chair is one of a pair. (*Mrs Hughes*)

253. Two papier mâché chairs, with cane seats. (*Left*) Chair with painted floral decoration. (*Right*) Chair with a painted panel in the back protected by glass. The panel incorporates mother of pearl partially painted, which creates an effect of changing light. (*Mrs Hughes*)

255. Papier mâché circular table with tripod base. The top, inlaid with mother of pearl, is a chess board. (*Mrs Hughes*)

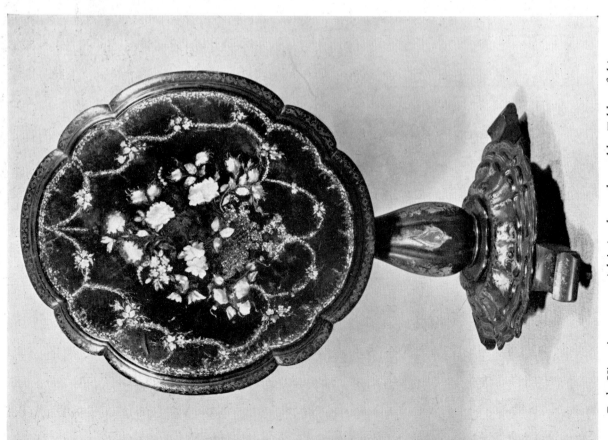

254. Early Victorian paper mâché circular or loo table. Tables of this type often had a solid metal rod fixed inside the centre pillar to take the weight. In this example large pieces of mother of pearl have been cleverly shaped and placed to simulate flowers. (*Mrs Hughes*)

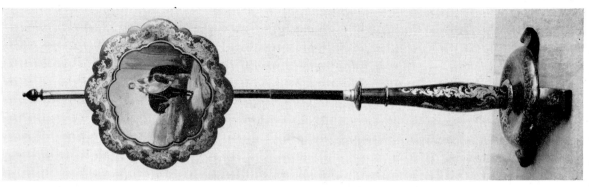

256. Papier mâché teapoy painted with rich floral decoration. Peacocks were popular with papier mâché decorators and can often be seen incorporated in the design. (*Victoria and Albert Museum*) 257. (*Left*) Papier mâché firescreen, on a tripod base, incorporating a needlework panel. (*Right*) Small table, which portrays Melrose Abbey on the top; the decoration is carried out in mother of pearl with a few touches of gold paint. The entire lighting effect and perspective is achieved by the placing of the mother of pearl so that the grain runs in different directions. (*Mrs Hughes*) 258. Papier mâché pole screen. It is believed that the picture depicts one of Queen Victoria's daughters on horseback. (*Victoria and Albert Museum*)

259. Elaborately shaped papier mâché music rack, incorporating a drawer in the frieze. (*Victoria and Albert Museum*)

260. Dwarf break-front book case. Instead of the more conventional grilles or glass doors, there are papier mâché panels; the peacock, popular with decorators, is incorporated in the design. (*Pelham Galleries*)

261. Bentwood armchair and single chair made by Thonet of Vienna. These chairs were sold in great quantities in England throughout the last half of the 19th century. They were both strong and light and many remain today. (*Mrs Hammond*)

262. Label of Thonet of Vienna pasted to the seat rail of one of the chairs (Fig. 261). (*Mrs Hammond*)

263. Drawing for sofa made about 1830, which still retains some of the features of the Regency. It is possible that the seat incorporated springs, although the general outline of the upholstery has been kept fairly tailored and clean cut.

264. Two sofas illustrated in a pre-Victorian catalogue of William Smee & Sons, Finsbury Pavement, London. Although other illustrations in the same catalogue show lightly buttoned upholstered furniture, it was not until the 1840s that deep buttoning became the vogue and was adopted almost universally.

265. Design for a sofa drawn by Thomas H. Kendall, who has shown two alternative designs for the back; on the left the upholstery is enclosed by a polished carved wood frame, but on the right there is a simple rolled upholstered edge. This sketch is undated, although it was probably drawn soon after 1859 when Kendall started his business; at this date, however, the style had been current for at least fifteen years.
(D. W. Kendall, Esq.)

266. Early Victorian
sofa at Sheringham
Hall, Norfolk. The deep
buttoning so popular at
this date can clearly be
seen here.
(*Thomas Upcher, Esq.*)

267. Sofa with a deeply
buttoned back, but
without arms. If the
seat had been repeated
on the other side of the
back, Victorians would
have called it an otto-
man. The design of this
piece suggests that it may
well have been one of
a pair which were inten-
ded to be placed back to
back, thus giving the ap-
pearance of an ottoman.
(*Philip Blairman, Esq.*)

268 and 269. (*Left*) Upholstered armchair made about 1840 and somewhat similar to one illustrated in Smee's catalogue (Fig. 277). This chair has been re-upholstered and no doubt the buttoning was originally deeper. (*Philip Blairman, Esq.*) (*Right*) Rosewood upholstered chair. (*Mrs Hammond*)

270 and 271. (*Left*) One of a pair of rosewood spoon-backed tub chairs. This example is identical to the pair shown in the illustration of the Queen's Retiring Room (Fig. 276). The upholstery of this chair, however, has been renewed in recent years and no doubt the original cover had deep buttoning. (*George J. Levy, Esq.*) (*Right*) 'Prie-dieu' or kneeling chair. Chairs of this design were popular throughout the early and mid-Victorian periods. (*Mrs Ronald Whineray*)

272 and 273. (*Left*) Typical small rosewood mid-Victorian spoon-backed upholstered chair. (*Philip Blairman, Esq.*) (*Right*) Another somewhat similar example of the same type of chair. (*C. F. Wearn*)

274 and 275. (*Left*) Small upholstered occasional chair with legs of rosewood. The upholstered back is of an unusual shape with the edge deeply serrated. (*Philip Blairman, Esq.*) (*Right*) 'Prie-dieu' or kneeling chair. The covering has recently been renewed, although the deep buttoning and heavy fringe now on the chair must closely resemble the original upholstery. (*Mallet & Son*)

276. The Queen's Retiring Room at the Crystal Palace; one of twenty-five coloured plates issued in a folder entitled *Recollections of the Great Exhibition* and published by Lloyd Bros. in September, 1851. The illustration shows five different types of chair and a sofa; all the upholstery is deeply buttoned and its use in the Queen's Retiring Room confirms that it was high fashion at this date.

277. Illustrations from William Smee & Sons' catalogue, issued about 1840. Both are described as 'superior lounge chairs'.

278. Large, thickly upholstered sofa at Stradey Castle, Carmarthenshire. The covering is of velvet incorporating large panels of oriental carpet. No wooden parts are visible and the feet and seat rail are entirely covered with velvet upholstery and a deep elaborate fringe. (*C. R. Mansel Lewis, Esq.*)

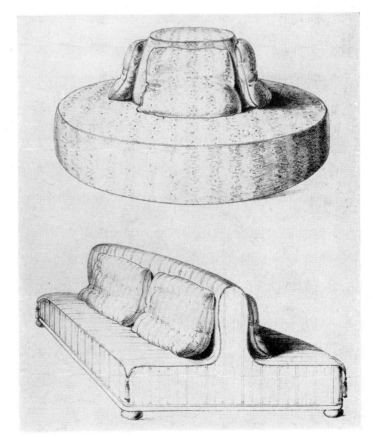

279. Designs for two early Victorian ottomans. Until about the mid-1840s these pieces of furniture were simple in outline with very little, if any, of the woodwork frame showing. Later examples became more elaborate (Fig. 65). This was often taken to extremes when the centres of circular ottomans were surmounted by woodcarving, statuary, an elaborate lamp or even a jardinière.

280. Tête-à-tête, with deeply buttoned upholstery; the legs and table are of ebonised wood picked out in gold. This piece, at Ragley Hall, Warwickshire, is a comfortable and ingenious method of seating two people and also of enabling them to have somewhere to put their tea or other refreshment. (*Marquess of Hertford*)

281. Illustration of a tête-à-tête sofa from an early Victorian book of designs, somewhat similar to the example above. The shape of this sofa and the provision of a centre table was the sort of novelty that found particular favour with the Victorians.

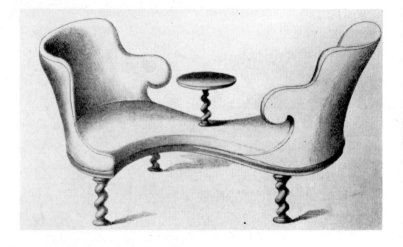

282. Fauteuil made by Filmer & Son of London and exhibited at the Paris Universal Exhibition of 1867. This piece is so constructed that it will divide into a sofa and four easy chairs. A writer in the *Art Journal Catalogue of the Exhibition* says: 'The plan is most ingenious, simple, and of manifest utility.'

Index

Figures in parentheses refer to illustration pages

Index

Index